❧ Acknowledgements ❧

This is a book that has been created with the loving support and guidance of many people throughout my life. While the focus of The Accountability Revolution is based on my most recent work during the past 15 years, it represents the learning and teaching I have received from many people since I was a youngster growing up.

First, I thank my Dad, Michael Samuel and my Mom, Meta Samuel, who are no longer with us in the physical world, but who live on in their teaching that I should try to do new things even in the face of opposition and to persevere past the frustrations, disappointments and mistakes along the way. I appreciate them for providing me loving support throughout my life and making sure that I never lost touch with my family, with music and with my heart.

I thank my daughter Sarah, who continues to inspire me through her loving, her fun, and her brilliant view of the world. I appreciate Nancy Grossman-Samuel for her loving support and belief, and her dedication to caring for our customers and our employees. I thank Ivan Grossman for his encouragement, guidance and continued support, especially during those years when my business was struggling.

I appreciate Sophie Chiche as my loving partner, and for challenging me to new levels of personal transformation and self-acceptance. I appreciate Leah Miller, Sophie's daughter, for her zest and enthusiasm to participate in new adventures. I thank Laurent Chiche for being a model as a young, dedicated and creative business leader.

I thank John-Roger for his spiritual teaching and loving guidance that continues to move me toward greater levels of clarity and understanding, and for providing experiences that I thought were impossible. I appreciate John Morton for his spiritual guidance, his loving support, and his model as a courageous leader in continual transformation.

I thank my extended family, which has supported me through many years of growth and development and provided me continual inspiration. I thank Sylvia Novak for always encouraging me to live my dreams. I thank Sandi and Paul Caplan for their loving inspiration and their model as business and community leaders. I thank Davee Gunn and Rita Giachini who have not only been a great model of success, but who have also been a model for enjoying life at the same time.

There have been several mentors and coaches in my life. I thank Newton Margulies, Ph.D. for inspiring me into the field of Organization Development and providing me the encouragement, support and foundational skills to be an effective consultant. I thank Bob Newcomb, Ph.D. for teaching me to go outside the box as a teacher and to get involved in anything that mattered to me. I thank Drs. Ron and Mary Hulnick for creating and leading the University of Santa Monica, which is the finest example of education that inspires and guides people (me) to new depths of personal transformation. Most recently, I thank Richard Barrett for his inspiration and guidance in writing a book that would make a difference. I thank Tracy Quinton, Dr. Cheryl Malakoff, Norm Frye and Beverly Berg for their outstanding coaching, counseling and friendship. I thank Marty Brotman,

M.D. for his belief in me, for instilling within me a confidence that anything is possible and for assisting me to approach life with a positive focus.

There are business leaders who continue to inspire me through their dedication to success and their drive to make a difference in their community and for their employees. Thanks to Jim Lussier, CEO of St. Charles Medical Center; Martin Babinec, CEO of TriNet VCO; Bob Barber, Ph.D., President of Central Oregon Community College; Jack McCredie, Associate Vice Chancellor Information Systems & Technology for the University of California, Berkeley; John Jones, Ph.D., President of Organizational Universe Systems; Lee Kaiser, Ph.D., creator of the Healing Healthcare Movement; Art Ushijima, CEO of Queen's Medical Center; Richard Chang, CEO of Richard Chang & Associates; Drew Childs, CEO of ORMOC Solutions; Tom McGuiness, Senior Vice President, Citrus Valley Health Partners; Dennis Morgan, President of Morgan Marketing Group; Dan Struve, President of Helpmates Personnel Services; Michael Brandman, CEO of Michael Brandman Associates; and Hayley Ditzler, President of Louth Automation.

There are several people who have been in the field of organization development who have been my teachers in one way or another. I thank Chip Clitheroe for his loving friendship and guidance during my formative years in this field. I thank the many consultants who have worked with me and contributed to the development of the concepts and understanding presented in this book, including David Rodgers, Todd Alexander, Richard Noble, John Hamerski, Dan Hogan, Sherry Bender, Jamie Woolf, Sondra Ford, Ph.D., Allan Matos, Luis Manuel Ramirez, Lois Vallerga, Nancy Moore, Teresa Edmondson, Charlie Hedges, Teresa Roche, Nancy Young, Ph.D., Carolyn Yates, Paul Henry, Minna Graham, Marc Croteau, Joan Pastor, Ellen Eiseman, Mary

Wayne Bush, Marilyn Parker, Steve Grossman, Jane Grossman, Vivette Payne, Tom Carey, Marilyn Kobb, Linda Watkins, Ph.D., Robert Mehler, Patrick Carmichael, Leslie Boyer, Sally Hedges, Annette Shaked, Joan Ritchie, Lynn Timerman, Jack McLellan, Dorothy Weber, Tim Manning, Merv Donner, Tim Stalder, Jean-Marie Hamel, Ph.D., Ginny Krekling, Ira Needleman, Judy Issokson, Tom Glymph, Nicole and Frank Becker, Deborah Berzan, Brenda Raine, Dina Zvenko, Wendy Maxwell, Kathy Rau, Kimberlee Walsh, Mike Sanders, Bob Ricioli, and Connie Stomper, Ph.D.

This book was a labor of love for several years. With deepest gratitude, I thank Barbara Novak for her consistent support, her loving encouragement during times of struggle, her belief in me when I doubted myself, and her skill and contribution to this book. I thank Laren Bright, who took a well-written book and polished it in a way that brought it to life. I thank Judi Goldfader for her brilliance in turning my manuscript into a beautiful book along with her team of top professionals who made it happen with unbelievable speed and excellence.

I thank Glenn Hays and the IMPAQ team, including Michael Phillips, Andrea Braun, Teresa Wong, Therese Skrenes, and Carla Phillips who are dedicated to supporting IMPAQ's clients and me, and who worked hard to develop this book into a finished product.

I thank God for my health, my creativity and my opportunity to contribute.

Mark Samuel

Contents

❦ List of Figures ❧

∾ **Introduction** ∾

Achieve
Breakthrough Results

R evolutionary times require revolutionary solutions and
breakthrough results. These are times when we must
achieve "the impossible" in order to survive. This requires a different mindset. Can you imagine experiencing
downsizing and **increasing morale** at the same time? How many
times have you seen organizations **increase productivity** during
restructuring? When was the last time you read in the newspaper
that two merging organizations actually **increased performance
and customer service?** Not only are these results possible, but
the organizations that plan to thrive in the next millennium are
achieving those results today.

I'm not just talking through my hat. Here are some of the
results I have personally measured:

- A division of TRW in Orange, California reduced turnover
  from a staggering 21% to a respectable 6%, and they did it
  within 6 months.

- A nursing unit at St. Charles Medical Center in Bend, Oregon **decreased their paralyzing 30% of management's time spent dealing with team conflicts to a marginal 2%** in less than one year. In addition, a department experienced the impossible: **During three months of downsizing and restructuring—typically a dismal time for morale— morale actually *increased* along with performance.**

- With Mervyn's of California in Hayward, California two district teams **improved from being rated the lowest in performance to receiving the highest performance rating** after just 6 months.

And the examples go on and on. Why were these results achieved? Because there were no other options in order to survive. These organizations had to find a way to achieve unexpected results. That way was accountability.

When a company develops a culture of accountability, employees automatically respond to challenging situations in a positive, productive, and profitable way, no matter what changes the business environment throws at them!

This is a far cry from the cover-your-butt consciousness that pervades a world in which you never know if your job will be there tomorrow. However, the concept of mutual reliance is consistently proving itself to pay big dividends.

The Accountability Revolution shows how to lead your business so it remains effective, competitive and successful in the face of continual pressure to perform at higher levels. This book gives you practical strategies and tools used by leading organizations in diverse industries to achieve breakthrough results in half the time expected.

If You Can't Keep Up, You Won't Survive

Since the early 1980s, we have been experiencing a revolution in business more far-reaching than any other in history—even more profound in many ways than the Industrial Revolution.

It started with massive downsizing in almost every industry from manufacturing and retail to health care and government. It was all the more traumatic because the downsizing took place at every organizational level, from the bottom to the top, from line workers to executives. It has even extended to companies that once prided themselves on offering lifelong security to their employees.

At practically the same time, the global marketplace emerged and companies' overseas sales were suddenly exceeding those from their traditional domestic customers. Meanwhile, high technology was enabling third world countries, like India, to enter the marketplace and claim a significant percentage of high tech based jobs. Add to the mix mergers of enormous institutions like Bank of America and Nations Bank as well as global mergers like that of Chrysler and Daimler which began changing the face of business forever.

The latest kick in the pants is the commercial application of the Internet. Its impact on every aspect of personal and professional life can't even begin to be imagined yet. How can any company prepare for a world that is literally different when you roll up the shades in the morning than it was when you turned out the lights the night before?

Managing Change Isn't Enough

Organizations today have to accomplish what was thought impossible ten years ago, and they usually have about six months to do it. Yet they must do it just to survive the massive resource cuts, the rising expectations of customers and to keep up with increasing competition. As a result, we have seen programs like Total Quality and Re-engineering—which have been attempts to keep up with the adaptations necessary to evolve organizations.

While important for continuous improvement, these approaches fail to match the speed at which organizations demand results. As Jack Welch is quoted in the book *"Jack Welch Speaks"* by Janet Lowe, "Speed is everything…Speed keeps businesses and people young."[1] We have come to rely on strategic planning and goal setting, only to find that people are adding more and more priorities to their plates before they are accomplishing their old ones.

We thought the focus on competencies would solve the problem, but found that competencies are changing as fast as the new business environment, so we still can't keep up. **We are going from one flavor-of-the-week change to another and spending more time on activities that produce change. But they do not provide bottom-line-enhancing results.**

The problem is that these management strategies are based on antiquated methods and thinking that worked in the good old days (fifteen years ago!), and no longer work today. We must shift from meaningless activity—like endless meetings, committees and email—to meaningful action where we make decisions that move the organization forward. **We must shift from improving processes to improving execution.** We must attack our organizational bad habits such as ignoring non-performers at the expense of hard working top producers. It is only when we have the courage to stop hiding from our ineffective functioning that we

---

[1] Janet Lowe, *Jack Welch Speaks: Wisdom from the World's Greatest Business Leader,* John Wiley & Sons, Inc., 1998.

can begin to address the real issues in today's fast-paced business environment.

We Can't Achieve High Performance without Accountability

When there is a lack of accountability, we don't get information when we need it, decisions aren't made when action is required, and people don't receive guidance or support when faced with new challenges.

When there is no accountability, non-performers thrive while the rest of us do double work picking up the slack. When there is no accountability, communication breaks down, territorialism increases, and recognition for success disappears. When there is no accountability, we fall into a victim mode of fighting each other, rebelling against change, and protecting ourselves at the cost of hurting others—and the company! How can you possibly achieve high performance under these circumstances, regardless of re-engineering, ISO or any other process improvement?

People are stressed by the effort needed to keep up with endless changes being made in organizations. But more importantly, they are burned out by the lack of accountability in the workplace where they have to work twice as hard to make up for those who aren't accountable. This nightmare has to stop—for the sake of all employees and the survival of our businesses.

True Accountability—Creating the Impossible

The word accountability usually conjures up pictures of a room full of people, all ducking behind their chairs and pointing their fingers at someone else, shouting, "It's their fault!" However, this has nothing to do with being accountable. In fact, if you are using accountability in response to a mistake or problem, it is too late! What's more, people who use accountability as a way to blame others are only hiding in a "victim" mode and avoiding their own involvement.

In my view, **accountability means that people can "count on one another" to keep performance commitments and communication agreements.** In an accountable organization, people ask for support when it is needed rather than waiting until there is a crisis that causes a major breakdown. Ultimately, employees are not only supported when they ask for assistance, but employees troubleshoot problems as if they *all* owned the problem, not just the affected individual(s).

Accountability is the basis for having an environment of trust, support and dedication to excellence. With accountability we can all depend on each other, and we don't have to worry about doing extra work because others failed to keep their agreements.

When people are accountable to each other, the resulting synergy creates new solutions that no one person could have developed. When people are accountable, they implement good solutions effectively. Many times, they accomplish their results in half the time expected, because of the participation and commitment of everyone as a team. When there is accountability, people feel supported during the most difficult times, whether it is dealing with a work related situation or a personal challenge that, even peripherally, affects their work. If you want to find an example of an accountable organization, look for any winning baseball team, dance company, symphony orchestra or any organization that is exceeding expectations against all odds.

Accountability is Power!

When I was getting my Masters degree in Management, it was often suggested that information was power. Even today, I hear about people who hoard information as a way of gaining influence. However, when I graduated, one of my mentors, Charlie Brotman, shared with me these words of advice. He told me, "If you want to rise in any career or in any organization, having information is important, but it doesn't give you power unless you do something with it. If you want to gain influence, you must be accountable. If people can depend on you for results, they will come to you when they need help. They will come to you when they need support because they will gain confidence in you based on your results. They will ask you for information, even if they know you don't have it, because they know you will get the information in a timely manner. When you are accountable, people can trust you because you keep your word. And when you can't, you are up front with them. Be accountable, and you will automatically be successful!"

Can you imagine promoting anyone who is not accountable? Accountability is clearly the single most important characteristic for increasing someone's responsibilities in the workplace—you must be able to count on them for getting results. In fact, your top performers are inevitably those who you can count on to achieve their business goals while supporting other team members. Whether you are developing managers to be better leaders and coaches, or you are developing employees to improve customer service and critical thinking, you must instill accountability to transform learning into performance and performance into results.

Accountability is the primary value for promoting individuals into positions of leadership and greater responsibility. And, accountability equates to job security.

Cadence Design Systems, a software company in San Jose, California, experienced their first major lay-off in company history. During that process, 30% of one department's employees were laid off. **Not one person who was trained in accountability was laid off, regardless of their position in that department.**

Unfortunately, many managers give "lip-service" to accountability but don't really support it. They include accountability as a stated Value for their organization, but don't take actions consistent with their commitments. They sabotage their credibility and their performance. This behavior was illustrated in a joke a friend sent to me over the Internet:

> *Two big companies, Company A and Company B, staged a boat race. Company A's team won by a mile.*
>
> *The managers of Company B wanted to find the reason for the crushing defeat, so they hired a consulting firm.*
>
> *The consultants noticed that Company A had eight people rowing and one steering. The Company B boat had one rower and eight people steering.*
>
> *After a year of study and millions spent on analysis, the consultants concluded that too many people were steering and not enough were rowing on the Company B team. So, before the next race, the Company B team was restructured; four steering managers, three area steering managers, and a new performance review system for the rower.*
>
> *This time the Company A team won by two miles.*
>
> *Company B fired the rower for poor performance and gave the managers a bonus for discovering the problem.*

While it's fun to laugh at a hypothetical company's ridiculous response, that very behavior is exactly what some of us have been trained to do; make changes that look great on paper but don't come close to producing the stated objective.

Accountability is Not an Option for Achieving and Sustaining Success—It's a Necessity

Unlike many change efforts that have come and gone, proving to be merely empty fads, accountability is neither a fad nor a change that can be ignored. We have clients who have experienced major improvements in performance using accountability. Some described in this book have received national awards and have achieved their highest levels of profitability. They have grown larger and stronger than anticipated and have improved their performance beyond expectations. Most of these organizations experienced a time of "comfort" with their stellar performance, which was not at all positive. As a result of resting on their laurels, their accountability diminished. They stopped looking for bad habits. They stopped checking their measurable variances in performance. They stopped addressing their unresolved conflicts and they stopped dealing with non-performers. As a result, their performance plummeted and they had to re-establish their accountability processes and commitments to get back on track.

The good news was that when they returned to their accountability practices they quickly became more successful again. This time, they had to increase their level of accountability, because the old level was no longer enough to sustain results. When accountability is an on-going process, excellence in performance naturally increases.

At IMPAQ®, we teach accountability, we hire individuals who are accountable and we maintain streamlined processes based on accountability. As a result, we achieved 25% growth rates several years in a row. However, we got accustomed to our growth and became comfortable with our level of accountability. We found that believing in accountability wasn't enough. We almost lost our business because we took our eye off the ball and stopped looking for ways to measure our business, surface our bad habits and confront our comfort zone. Luckily, we recovered and are now experiencing our strongest growth ever.

The 7 Deadly Sins that Prevent Us from Achieving Results

Sin #1: Over-Assessment

We conduct assessments and re-assessments to make sure that our proposal to improve results is in the right area. Sometimes this takes the form of benchmarking and other times climate surveys. Regardless, many organizations fail to be responsive to the demands of their customers or the needs of their employees due to the habit of continual assessment without ever taking action.

Sin #2: Plan to Perfection

We want our plan to be perfect in hopes that we can make the naysayers comfortable with it so that they won't be negative when it is implemented. We also hope that a perfect plan will lead to perfect implementation so we won't feel guilty when chaos and crises occur. In trying to ensure that everyone remains comfortable by being involved in the change, we end up fostering conflict and confusion that leads to even greater resistance. By the time the plan is implemented, our lack of responsiveness during the planning process increases the pressure to achieve results.

Sin #3: Communicate for Buy-In

We are so invested in people feeling comfortable with the new plan that we take months to communicate it. We make our presentation "nice and pretty," selling the program to ensure that everyone will like it. Then, when people resist in spite of our sales pitch, we either change our message to appease them, causing a lack of credibility, or we commit the first Sin once again by conducting yet another reassessment, which delays implementation even further.

Sin #4: Empower Instead of Guide

We have become so concerned with our own comfort that we empower others to effect the plan, abdicating our own involvement as managers or leaders. Some managers don't even bother to undertake any planning before empowering their employees. They are generally the same ones who punish their people when they fail, but never make any attempt to coach their people to success. Other managers empower employees after the plan is complete. Unfortunately, we are better at planning a strategy than we are at planning its execution. This leaves employees feeling abandoned and directionless, resulting in even greater confusion and conflict.

Sin #5: Avoid Monitoring Progress

No one wants to face "bad news," so we avoid monitoring our progress. That way we don't run the risk of discovering we aren't on track for success. Neither do we find ourselves in the uncomfortable position of having to monitor the progress of others, which might put us in a situation where we would need to coach them, resolve conflicts and problems, or admit to upper management that we have gone off track. However, by not monitoring progress, we may stray even further off track without knowing it and diminish the likelihood of recovery.

Sin #6: Fail to Recognize Success

Because we haven't monitored our progress, we have no way of recognizing success. If we can't even determine whether the plan was successful, we can't possibly acknowledge people for their contributions. So we don't. We speed on to the next program, leaving people frustrated, with no sense of completion or acknowledgement for their hard work. As a result, we not only have a failed effort—we have demoralized employees.

Sin #7: Avoid Holding People Accountable

We establish no consequences for those who are sabotaging the success of the team and the organization. This is usually because of our desire to be fair, to give everyone a chance to be heard and to make everyone comfortable with the plan. Certainly the prospect of overwhelming new responsibilities may cause anyone to resist even the most positive changes. It may be appropriate, even constructive, to resist a new plan when it is first discussed or implemented. This is when a devil's advocate position may still be helpful. However, when someone resists a plan well after it has been implemented and the new norms have been established, it undermines the success of the plan and demoralizes those who are trying to make it work. We have all witnessed the failure of a program after its initial success due to a group of negativists who never gave the plan a chance to work. They are actually empowered to sabotage because there are no penalties to discourage them.

Ultimately, I discovered that managers take a lot of time to plan and implement in a way that makes everyone feel comfortable, only to find that they have all but destroyed their organization and its people in the process.

Anatomy of Accountability

Over the years, I have identified six elements that are present in an accountability-based® culture.

1. ***Clear Intention.*** In order to accomplish something, you need to know just what you want to accomplish. It must be clearly defined. This isn't a goal statement, but a clear picture of success stated as a result. This includes *what* the desired outcome is and approximately *when* it is to be accomplished.

2. ***Interlocking Ownership.*** Once everyone involved knows what is needed—whether they agree with it or not—each person must deal with their part of the project as if they owned the entire project. This means taking it beyond merely getting the job done. It means following the intention of the project, not just the letter of the plan, and giving 100% of what they have to offer. This is demonstrated through interdependence and integrating people, process and skills to produce the stated result. An amazing

synergy takes place when all parties step forward and produce at this level—and everyone wins!

3. ***Effective Execution.*** This means you assassinate anyone who messes up. No, wait, that's the old model of accountability. Execution is the process of linking people and processes to achieve high performance. It is represented by the qualities of coordination, timing, communication, decision making and actions necessary to achieve desired outcomes. While often thought of as the "soft side" of performance, execution is often practiced and rehearsed by the best professional performing groups whether in the field of drama, music, sports or dance. Ultimately, execution determines whether you succeed or fail in accomplishing your desired actions.

4. ***Relentless Attack of Dysfunctional Habits.*** We all have bad habits that keep us from accomplishing our goals. Generally, we maintain these habits to stay comfortable instead of going through the struggle, discipline and sometimes the pain of correcting a bad situation. For instance, we avoid conflicts, we avoid dealing with non-performers and we avoid measuring our performance. We conduct lots of assessments and still never address the real issues that prevent success. However, the accountable leader makes it a point to surface and address dysfunctional habits.

5. ***Responsive Recovery.*** Projects rarely (okay, never) go exactly as planned. Knowing that, success becomes a matter of being prepared to handle inevitable glitches. Effective recovery requires that everyone involved be prepared to make corrections as they are needed during the project's execution. Many managers demand *perfection*— which tends to create a tension that almost ensures screw-ups. A better approach is to expect *excellence*, which lifts everyone to his/her highest level. When perfection is demanded, people will cover up their errors or non-production, and the consequences of that will invariably

show up at the worst possible time. When excellence is the objective, people know that, instead of being punished, they will be supported toward success if problems arise. So they automatically have the freedom—even incentive—to ask for help as soon as it's needed, thus avoiding ship-wrecks.

6. ***Ruthless Measuring of Results.*** In order to know whether you have been successful, you need to know not only what you accomplished, but also how well you accomplished it. It is the lack of preparing to adequately measure results that undermines many companies. Without measuring results, you don't know whether you are on track or off. Some people will often feel discouraged after a change has been implemented, since they feel it didn't work as well as it should. However, they may find that the results of the change are good once results have been assessed. Others are happy accomplishing changes and feel really good about how well the changes were implemented. But until they measure their results, they don't realize that they didn't address the real problems and accomplish bottom-line improvements. When there are measurable results, good performance can be noted and rewarded. Everyone involved knows his or her part was critical to the success, and everyone benefits from the reward.

When people are accountable, they work together to implement good solutions. Everyone participates and is committed to a known and measurable outcome. The resulting synergy produces greater results—very meaningful results—in significantly less time.

One of my favorite examples of team accountability involved a group of line workers at Pacific Bell. One of the team members described with great pride his team's impact on the organization.

This team had its resources diminished when the organization was experiencing major cut backs and eventual downsizing.

Instead of becoming victim to the cuts, this team decided on their own (without intervention from a consultant, including myself), that they would rise above the cuts and increase their performance and productivity without additional resources. This is their story told in terms of the process of accountability described earlier:

1. ***Clear Intention.*** At one of their team meetings, a team member led the group to create an intention of becoming the best functioning team in the organization during this crisis period. They observed the whining and complaining of others in the organization regarding the budget cuts and created the clear intention to remain positive, supportive, and to strive for high performance. They pictured their team as highly effective, sharing resources, supporting one another to accomplish the desired outcomes, and conducting their own effort to improve processes and reduce costs. Ultimately, they saw themselves as a high-performing team where they recognized each other's successes, developed each other's skills, and distanced themselves from those outside of the team who were more negative.

2. ***Interlocking Ownership.*** Before they left the meeting they made sure that everyone on the team agreed to put the team's needs above their own individual needs. This didn't mean that they would ignore individual issues. In fact, if an individual had a problem, he or she would bring it up to the team for support, rather than remaining silent. They agreed to review their commitment once a month to make sure they were on track.

3. ***Effective Execution.*** They took it upon themselves to improve their coordination, communication and productivity by reviewing their processes and the way in which they were performing their jobs. It turned out that their processes were fairly streamlined, but they were wasting resources by not sharing more and by not communicating

their activities with others. This was improved and their costs went down.

4. ***Relentless Attack of Dysfunctional Habits.*** After about 6 months, they discovered differences in performance between some of the members. As a team, they decided to address those disparities in a supportive way, rather than ignoring the problem. They discovered that the two individuals involved needed some training, which they provided through cross-training.

5. ***Responsive Recovery.*** After about 9 months, the equipment they were using broke during the night shift. Because they already had a recovery process in place, they were able to get other necessary team members to come in during the night shift and clean up the mess to minimize the impact of the breakdown. Also, they immediately held a meeting to discuss alternatives for replacing the equipment and getting back on track.

6. ***Ruthless Measuring of Results.*** At the end of the year, they reviewed their performance improvements and accomplishments. They identified cost reductions through better use of resources, greater customer responsiveness as a result of having become more efficient, and faster recovery time when breakdowns occurred.

About six months after making their report of improvement, an executive in the organization attended one of their team meetings. He congratulated the group for their effort and contribution as a team. And while the rest of the organization was continuing to experience budget cuts, the executive asked the team what additional resources could make their jobs even more effective. He said, "You successfully demonstrated that we can trust you to make the best of your situation and achieve meaningful results. Therefore, we want to support you in doing more of that in the future."

Leading the Revolution

Since I believe this is a time of revolution, not evolution, it is also a time of heroes. Who are the heroes in today's revolution? You can be. Heroes start out as ordinary people who see what is necessary, and begin doing it, even if by current measure it is considered extraordinary. *The Accountability Revolution* **provides all you need to know to become a hero, to produce the results, to survive, prosper, and take your associates along with you.**

The way is clear. It may not be easy, but you can do it. It requires making the tough decisions that keep organizations progressing. You must surface the problems that prevent success and facilitate solutions rather than abdicating your role under the guise of empowering your people.

Part of the process is asking yourself whether everything you do or assign to others is meaningful action or just pointless activity. That means eliminating unproductive meetings and coaching non-performers who are sabotaging success—and morale. It requires developing skills to lead with a greater sense of urgency, clearer strategy, and a higher level of responsiveness.

In short, it involves being more accountable and creating more accountability within the work environment so employees experience being supported.

Part I of this book, *Break Away from Old Leadership Paradigms*, challenges widely used leadership practices and reveals the breakdowns and victimization that results from these practices. It replaces the myths with "truths of leadership" that foster organization-wide accountability and catapult performance to new standards of excellence.

Part II, *Five Strategies for Leading with Accountability*, provides the essential systems and tools for developing a culture of accountability and leadership for results. Implementing these strategies will produce a highly spirited work force that achieves more, does it faster, and experiences breakthroughs in quality performance and sustained desired results.

It is our responsibility as managers to effectively hold the vision of success and to support the steps necessary to achieve it. We must continually pioneer new frontiers to provide our people with the best environment for meeting the changing demands of business.

The Accountability Revolution represents the beginning of this journey into a new paradigm of results-focused activity. However, we must have the courage to let go of those parts of our old paradigm that are no longer effective. We must have the courage to take risks, to continue on our path of self-improvement, and to follow our truths as we experience our relationship to an ever-changing society.

If we are going to survive in the future, we must find ways to operationalize and integrate accountability as a core value. We must create an environment where we can count on one another and, most of all, where we can count on ourselves to achieve our desired outcomes.

∞ **Part 1** ∞

Break Away
from Old Leadership Paradigms

➠ Unleash Ability
Through Accountability

➠ Create an Accountable Culture:
Stop Avoiding the Real Issues!

➠ Break Three "Bad Habits"
of Ineffective Leadership

➠ The Formula
to Achieve Breakthroughs

➠ Leadership Roles
that Produce Breakthrough Results

∞ **1** ∞

Unleash Ability
through Accountability

Myth: Accountability is a way to blame someone for making a mistake, resulting in fear.

Truth: Accountability is the key for increasing trust, reducing fear, and improving morale and performance.

The hugely successful Dilbert comic strip clearly strikes a chord deep within the heart of corporate America. Much of its humor arises from the low levels of accountability within Scott Adams' mythical corporation, where management trainees are instructed to "Never be in the same room as a decision." There we encounter the Evil H.R. Director, who reminds the boss to be sure to avoid contact with subordinates. A quick tour of the Dilbert website produces this gem of corporate wisdom from The Center for Executive DUHcision-Making: "Informed decision-making comes from a long tradition of guessing and then blaming others for inadequate results."

We laugh, but by exposing the painful "truths" of the corporate world, exaggerated though they may be, Scott Adams has started us off on the road to recovery. Because to laugh at our weaknesses means to acknowledge them. And once we have acknowledged their existence we can begin to address them.

The Accountability Revolution offers a systematic approach to increasing organizational accountability. The same principles can be applied to increasing personal accountability, another rich source of contemporary humor. When Homer Simpson or a member of the former Seinfeld gang demonstrates an astonishing and all-too-human lack of integrity, then struggle to justify the unethical choices they've made, our laughter comes from the same well that it does when we read a Dilbert cartoon strip. But beneath the laughter is pain. The time has come to confront that pain and do something about it. We can begin by dismissing the myth that accountability is an "all or nothing behavior."

A CEO of a medium-sized high tech organization (Interstate Electronics) called me into his office and complained, "No one around here is accountable for anything. Everyone is busy, but no one is accountable!" I asked him what would be different if people were accountable. He responded, "Projects would get completed on time and within budget. If everyone would just take accountability and do their jobs, we would be successful."

Clearly, he viewed accountability as an all or nothing event. I asked, "If everyone was individually accountable and completed their own tasks but didn't coordinate their activities with project team mates, would projects get completed on time?

"No," he replied. "We would have to establish processes for people to work together in a project team. Then, they would be fully accountable."

I further asked him, "If each project team completed its tasks by coordinating with each other, but didn't share information with other project teams and functional departments, would your organization still be successful?"

Looking a little discouraged he responded, "No. We would have duplication of effort, wasted resources and delayed or poor decisions. If we are to be fully accountable and successful, people must complete their own tasks, coordinate amongst teammates, and share information with other project teams and functional departments."

"So it sounds like accountability is more than people just doing their jobs," I asked.

"Right," he agreed. "But if people aren't doing their own jobs, then the remaining parts of accountability can't happen."

I told him he was absolutely right, and added that everyone needs clear expectations, guidance and coaching in order to be successful and to be fully accountable. "So now," I said, "let's talk about how many people you have either coached or let go for non-performance."

With a look of shock, he responded, "None. I guess accountability begins with me."

The Five Levels of Accountability

Accountability is an evolutionary process that can have a revolutionary impact on an organization. There are distinct levels of organizational accountability with predictable characteristics at each level. Figure 1-1 details the range of accountability from "Entitlement" (no accountability) to "Organizational Accountability" (complete accountability).

Figure 1-1: The Accountability Continuum

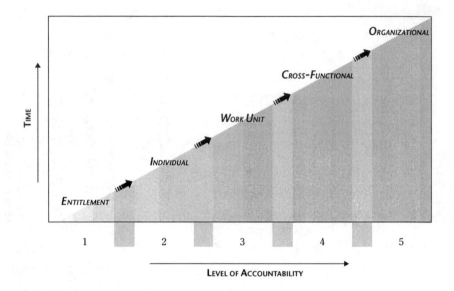

Within your organization you will find some managers and employees functioning below the normal levels of accountability, and others functioning at higher levels, so that if you were to chart the organization's level of accountability it would resemble a bell curve distribution.

Figure 1-2: Typical Accountability Levels in an Organization

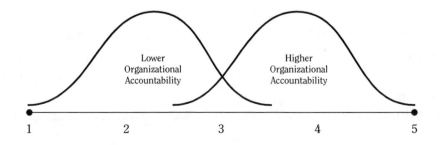

Level 1: Entitlement

One of my first jobs was working for Fairview State Hospital in California. I was given an assignment by the Hospital Administrator to gather information. I will never forget going to another department and asking for specific data I knew existed. The clerical administrator told me very politely that she had the data I was seeking, and then returned to her work without retrieving it for me. Surprised, I asked her if she was busy, or if there was some other problem. No, she wasn't really busy, and there was no problem. Then she picked up the phone and made a call to her sister. By this time, I was not only frustrated, but also furious about the lack of responsiveness. I waited for seven minutes, and then in exasperation I asked her if she would *please* get me the data I was requesting and explained the importance of the assignment to the Hospital Administrator. "No," she replied calmly. "It's not my job."

When an organization is plagued by an attitude of Entitlement, employees are paid for showing up on the job regardless of performance.[1] There are no expectations for performance and people are free to perform in any manner that is comfortable to them. Convenience determines effort. Ultimately, morale is low from the indifference that everyone has for their own performance and for each other's performance.

Level 2: Individual Accountability

The stage of Individual Accountability is an improvement on Entitlement. Here, employees take responsibility for completing

---

[1] Judith M. Bardwick presents a thought-provoking analysis of the dangers of entitlement in her book, *Danger in the Comfort Zone*, American Management Association, 1991.

their own assignments based on their own job descriptions, without concern for the impact they may have on others. People are competitive with their teammates and support is minimal. Consistency is low and fragmentation is high, creating a high degree of frustration. People have to work harder to improve their performance since they can depend only on themselves in isolation from the rest of the team and organization. Coordination of effort is low and results in poor utilization of resources. Decisions are made without regard for the impact on others on the team or within the organization.

Level 3: Work Unit Accountability

Teams are another stage on the route to organizational accountability. At this stage the success of the team is more important than any particular individual's success. People on the team assist each other in being successful. Competition among team members is lower; however, territorialism is still high. Coordination is high within the team, but is ineffective among functional areas, resulting in wasted human and technical resources. Teams deal with individual poor performance and behaviors that keep the team from being successful. Decisions are made without considering the impact on the rest of the organization.

Level 4: Cross-Functional Accountability

At this level of accountability, the business outcomes drive the makeup of the team to get the job done *regardless* of function. Decisions are made to include as many functions or departments as are affected. Achieving the outcome is more important than the success of any team or individual. Coordination among teams and individuals is very high. Territorialism doesn't exist and individual competition is minimal. Human and technical resources are shared effectively among functional areas based on need and urgency.

Level 5: Organizational Accountability

This level is similar to level 4 but represents a further refinement that the business outcomes drive the makeup of the team to get the job done regardless of function *or level* within the organization. Any person can be a lead to any other person in the organization based on the need for achieving the business outcome using people from all levels and functions. This level exemplifies the "fluid" organization that can adapt to any situation that arises. Organizations at this level of accountability also work with other organizations in collaborative partnerships to offer better services and products.

Using the table on the following page, identify the accountability level at which your organization is currently operating. Determine whether you are operating at the same level of accountability. If you are interested in conducting a more in-depth assessment of accountability for yourself or your organization, you can take the Situational Action Inventory™, developed by John Jones and Mark Samuel to assess individual accountability according to the Accountability Continuum. For more information contact us at *info@impaqcorp.com*.

Figure 1-3: Levels of Accountability

Level of Accountability	1. Entitlement	2. Individual Accountability
Cultural Characteristics	- Chaotic - Low Morale - Low Trust - Low Support - Apathetic/No Involvement - Minimal Communication - High Resistance to Change - Conflicts are personality oriented - Little Direction from Leadership - No Recognition for Results	- Low Support - High Resistance to change - Highly Competitive between Team Members - High Territorialsim - Conflicts driven by Competition - Power Driven - Communication is Fragmented - Fear of Reprimands - Low Involvement - Individuals are Recognized for Effort and Results
Performance Characteristics	- No Operational Standards - Policies aren't defined or maintained - Poor Performance Accepted - Coordination is Poor - Wasted Human/Technical Resources - Decisions aren't made - Projects are over-budget and over-time	- Policies are Maintained - Operational Procedures are defined, with Consequences - Poor Performance is Addressed - Coordination is Poor - Duplication of Human and Tech nical Resources - Decisions are Political and Position-Driven - Projects are over-budget and over-time - Breakdowns between Functional Areas and Line and between Mgmt and Employees - Individual Performance undermines Org'l Results

3. Work Unit Accountability	4. Cross-Functional Accountability	5. Organizational Accountability
- Support is High in Team - Medium level of Trust - Highly Competitive between functional teams and departments - Cross-Functional territorialism - Departmental Conflicts - Communication Fragmented - We/They Attitude - Medium Involvement - Individuals and Teams are not recognized for Results	- Confusion about Direction based on misinformation - Conflicts between levels within organization - Communication blocked - High involvement of Middle Management and non-management - High Support between functions and within teams - Medium to High Morale - Individuals and Teams are recognized for Results	- Clear Leadership Direction - High Communication and Information Flow - Decisions are made at all levels and include all functions - Direction is Clear and updated regularly - Conflicts resolved quickly - High Involvement of execs middle managers and non-mgmt in moving the org'n forward to achieve business outcomes - High Support between levels and functions and within Teams - High Morale from feeling of making meaningful accomplishments - Individuals and Teams are recognized for Results
- Policies are Maintained - Operational Procedures defined w/consequences - Poor Performance is addressed by team and leader - Resources aren't shared, causing duplication - Coordination between functional areas breakdown - Decisions don't include affected parties and need to be remade or fail - Global Projects are over-budget and over-time - Team Performance undermines Org'l Results	- Polices are Maintained - Operational Procedures are defined with consequences - Poor Performance handled by team & leader ... except at upper mgmt level where non-performance is tolerated - Resources are shared - Coordination between functional areas is high and seamless - Decisions include affected cross-functional parties, but may break down between levels - Projects are held up by lack of decisions from management - Org'l Performance is undermined by friction between levels in the organization	- Policies are Maintained - Operational Procedures are defined, with Consequences - Poor Performance is Addressed - Resources are Shared - Coordination is High and Seamless - Decisions include affected crosss-functional parties and appropriate levels of the organization - Projects are effectively monitored and decisions made at the appropriate levels to assure continuous progress - Org/l Performance is assured by the "fluid" involvement of the appropriate levels of the organization

Guidelines to Increase Organizational Accountability

1. In general, you must increase accountability one level at a time.

Back in 1994, at the height of "teams" as a popular change effort, I worked with an organization that decided moving to a team-based culture would increase performance in the organization. The problem was that up until that point, there had been no consequences for individual non-performance. For a while, the energy in the organization improved in response to the promise of working together in teamwork. However, after a few months, the non-performers still didn't perform, and now they blamed the team for the lack of results. Without the organization's strength to foster individual accountability, it was hard to maintain team-based accountability.

It takes about six months to a year to solidify each new level. However, in times of crisis, the organization's culture has an opportunity to skip a level of accountability. Unfortunately, this opportunity is rarely seized because people are more in-clined to revert to a *lower* level of accountability during a crisis, in the same way that people will often withdraw when they are in a state of fear. But once they determine that they are not at risk, they may then skip a level, exhibiting an unusual degree of accountability. We see this within communities when an earth-quake or some other natural disaster has occurred.

But apart from the unusual circumstances brought on by a crisis, skipping a level of accountability is rarely successful or lasting. One reason many Total Quality, Re-engineering or similar improvement programs fail to stick is that they ignore the evolution of accountability. That's why people who meet to solve problems as a cross-functional team often resume territorial behavior when they return to their work unit.

2. As levels of accountability increase, the number of both performance and behavioral expectations increase.

When I was 12 years old, I played on a little league team that was expected to win the championship. We had the best individual ball players of any team. Unfortunately, every team member wanted to be the "star" of the team. So batters would swing for home runs, infielders would run into each other trying to get to the ball first, and outfielders would overthrow the ball trying to throw runners out. Frustrated and probably embarrassed by the losses we experienced, the coach decided to practice us harder and concentrate on our catching, batting, and throwing skills. Yet, we still lost games because our attitude and behavior of trying to be the "stars" never changed. We not only needed to be accountable for performing our skills at the highest level, we also had to be accountable for communicating, coordinating and cooperating with one another at the highest levels if we were going to win games. By the time the coach figured out that our "star" attitude was the problem, the season was over. We ran out of time and ended the year with a losing record.

As levels of accountability increase, it becomes less acceptable to accomplish individual performance goals without considering the effect on other people in the organization who need to accomplish their goals. For instance, when there is cross-functional accountability, each person must communicate, coordinate and make decisions with people in other functions in order to accomplish the organization's goals.

3. *The further removed an individual is from the organization's current level of accountability, the greater the pressure will be for that person to leave the organization.*

This is true whether an individual's level of accountability is higher than or lower than that of the organization.

A friend of mine was involved in a rock band whose members smoked marijuana at rehearsals. My friend smoked marijuana as well. As time passed, my friend became aware of his addiction and decided to cut down. At the same time, the other band members started to experiment with cocaine. As my friend stopped smoking and the rest of the band members continued their experimentation, he found himself not fitting in with the band any longer and chose to leave.

∞ **2** ∞

Create an
Accountable Culture:
Stop Avoiding the Real Issues!

Myth: Culture affects people issues more than it affects business outcomes.

Truth: The achievement of business outcomes depends on the culture in which people work together to get results.

We need only look at the course of history to see that culture is anything but a "soft" issue. Whether we examine the decline of the Roman Empire or something more recent, such as the events in former Yugoslavia, the culture of a society plays a critical role in determining its health. We ignore it at our peril.

Within a few short years, Yugoslavia transformed from being a culture of toleration and mutual accommodation to being one of ethnic ghettoization. In 1984, Yugoslavia hosted the Winter Olympic Games at Sarajevo, an event that represents the highest level of tolerance and mutual acceptance among nations. Less than ten years later, Yugoslavia had become a battleground, and thousands of lives were destroyed in the name of "ethnic cleansing."

The problems that tore Yugoslavia apart were largely cultural ones. After World War I, Yugoslavia was created as a homeland for rival ethnic groups that had been conditioned by centuries of ethnic and religious hatreds. While these rivalries were rarely expressed under Communist rule, they continued to exist. The problems were never addressed with a view to solving them. Naturally, at the first opportunity—as soon as the Communist system failed—they burst forth, stronger and uglier and more violent than ever.

Culture: The Backbone of an Organization

Although traditionally we have treated organizational culture as a soft issue, it may be the single most important factor in an organization's ability to achieve its desired business outcomes. In the frustration of doing everything "right" and not achieving the desired results, we tend to initiate a frenzy of change efforts. We change our structure, re-engineer our systems, provide more training, do more planning, and still we fail to achieve the results we're after.

The culture of an organization involves more than the style, attitude, communication and skill of its managers and employees. The reason it has been treated as a soft issue is that it seems to affect people and morale more than it affects business results. Consequently, we debate which culture is best—team-based, self-directed, empowered, diverse, or something else—without reflecting on the primary purpose of any culture, which is to achieve the business outcomes. The problem is that we develop isolated programs to change the organizational culture in order to satisfy the "human element," while demanding harsh changes in the workplace, such as downsizing and cost cutting, in order to achieve our business results. The reality is that culture directly affects the organization's profitability and competitive edge in the marketplace to a degree that most people have failed to appreciate.

Unfortunately the cultures of most organizations today are based on a victim orientation of ignoring problems, blaming others for mistakes, rationalizing our inflexibility, resisting the need to change and/or improve, and hiding from those who are going to hold us accountable. Michael Hammer describes this well in his book, *Beyond Reengineering*, "Despite their many differences, there are great similarities across most contemporary corporate cultures. Certain themes resonate almost everywhere: Avoiding blame and responsibility, treating co-workers as competitors, feeling entitled, and not feeling intense and committed."[1]

The culture represents the fabric of the organization. You can't create a functional raincoat out of an evening gown without changing the fabric. It may look like a raincoat and it may be worn like a raincoat, but we have only to wear it out in the rain to know that it won't *function* as a raincoat. The same holds true for organizations. We can restructure our organization into teams, provide people with team awareness and skills through team training, and even change our compensation to a team-based structure, and still not have people *function* as a team that achieves the results we want.

Organizational culture is simply *the way people function together in order to achieve their desired business outcomes*. It

---

[1] Michael Hammer, *Beyond Reengineering: How the Process-Center is Changing Our Work and Our Lives,* Harper & Row, 1996.

involves more than the attitudes, skills and styles of people as individuals: it involves a mindset and the "patterns of behavior" supporting that mindset. It is as critical to the strategy of a high-performing organization as the decision to be a passing or a running team is to a high-performing football team. While a football team will establish its "plays" (the way the team members function together) in order to win, an organization must establish its ideal "patterns of behavior" in order to move towards its desired business outcomes. These "patterns of behavior" form the "hows" of the culture, as represented by some of the following processes:

- *How information is shared between levels and departments to ensure effective operations*

- *How coordination of activities is handled between departments*

- *How conflict is treated and addressed*

- *How decisions are made that impact various individuals and departments*

- *How non-performance is handled within a team and by management*

- *How people are developed according to the intention and future needs of the organization*

- *How people are recognized on a daily basis as opposed to "awards of the month"*

- *How problems are surfaced and quickly resolved.*

Effective "patterns of behavior" assist an organization in meeting customer needs, keeping costs low, supporting high productivity and assisting the organization in changing to achieve business outcomes. Examples of positive "patterns of behavior" and habits are:

- *Including the right people when making a decision to prevent breakdown or duplication of effort*

- *Coaching non-performers immediately with clear consequences to reduce the time spent in ineffective performance*

- *Communicating direction and change effectively to ensure swift action and involvement by those doing the implementing.*

Just as effective "patterns of behavior" support the organization's success, dysfunctional "patterns of behavior" undermine the organization's effectiveness and result in wasted resources, poor customer service, higher costs, lower productivity and inconsistent quality. Some of those dysfunctional "patterns of behavior" include:

- *Not surfacing project breakdowns when milestones aren't being met*

- *Not communicating expectations clearly, causing rework, wasted effort and a lack of responsiveness to customers*

- *Meetings that only share information, but where decisions aren't made and actions aren't taken to make progress on priorities.*

These "patterns of behavior" are generally automatic responses that people have in an organization regardless of position or function. As a result, they can be considered the "habits" of an organization. Dysfunctional habits represent the internal barriers of an organization. Most of the dysfunctional habits of an organization are based on fear and the absence of trust. Kathleen Ryan and Daniel Oestreich discuss the impact of fear in their book, *Driving Fear Out of the Workplace*, claiming, "We see fear as an increasingly visible background phenomenon that undermines the commitment, motivation, and confidence of people at work."[2] Fear undermines performance in a way that prevents organizations from achieving high performance and breakthrough results. It is the fear of making mistakes, of speaking out and being reprimanded for it, and of making others feel uncomfortable that causes breakdowns in coordinating projects, making critical decisions and taking initiative to solve problems that have surfaced. Developing an accountable organization means that we are constantly surfacing the dysfunctional "habits" of performance and communication, identifying the fear associated with those habits, and developing new "habits" that promote greater levels of trust and high performance.

While these "patterns of behavior" and "habits" appear to be the soft issues that affect only the morale, they are critical elements directly impacting the organization's performance, efficiency, reputation with customers and profitability. The real examples in Figure 2-1 illustrate the consequences of dysfunctional patterns of behavior, especially with regard to profitability.

Spineless Leadership Breeds Victimization

Just as it takes courage to tell the truth when we have to deliver "bad" news, it takes courage to lead with accountability. It is easy for managers to complain that employees aren't taking initiative, are wasting time on useless activities, are unwilling to put in the

---

[2] Kathleen D. Ryan and Daniel K. Oestreich, *Driving Fear Out of the Workplace,* Jossey-Bass, 1998.

effort to achieve excellence. However, when leadership doesn't have the courage to identify and articulate a clear direction for the future, demonstrated by the focus of a few priorities, employees waste time on meaningless activities and meetings, looking busy but not actually making progress. When leaders don't have the courage to make decisions, employees remain paralyzed either in conflict or awaiting approval. When leaders fail to demonstrate the courage to coach and deal with non-performers, employees quickly learn that hard work and dedication to excellence is neither respected nor recognized. When leaders don't demonstrate the courage to admit making mistakes, then employees also hide their mistakes and their failing projects. In addition, when leaders avoid addressing concerns, employees refuse to take continuous improvement, performance appraisal and professional development seriously. In general, when leadership runs away from taking accountability, employees respond in kind.

Old Habits Die Hard

A division of Lagoven,[3] a major petroleum company in Venezuela, needed to cut costs and improve its productivity in order to compete in the new global market. It was clear that in order to cut costs successfully, they had to share resources more effectively. Their management team decided that it was necessary to restructure the organization from centralized departments to cross-functional business units. This required changing the organization into a team-based culture. The previously autonomous departments—Maintenance, Operations, and Technical

---

[3] Now PDVSA

Figure 2-1: Dysfunctional Patterns of Behavior

Topic	Dysfunctional Pattern of Behavior	Result on Business Outcomes
Coordination in a BioMedical Organization	- Each Project Manager developed isolated plans for completing his or her part of the project without strategizing or coordinating plans with those involved in other parts of the project.	- Fragmented activities caused breakdowns that extended the completion of the project by over two years. The result was alate new product to market and millions of dallars in wastedresources, not to mention oportunity loss. **Note:** The project was scrapped and restarted with the same team of project managers. This time a new system of coordination was implemented when the project was initiated. the new product was developed ahead of the scheduled completion date.
Dealing with Non-Performers in a Financial Institution	- In support of a "polite" culture emphasizing "fairness" and comfort, there were no consequences for employees or managers who did not perform.	- Customer satisfaction dropped as competition increased resulting in reduced market share. In response to the need to reduce costs, a severance pkg was offered to employees and the org'n lost top performers who knew they could get a job elsewhere. The poorly-performing employees (concerened about their ability to find new work) stayed. This cost the org'n millions in lost market share, the expense of laying off employees, and the loss of customer confidence and satisfaction. **Note:** An electronics firm facing the same dilemma of poor performance, announced that performance/customer satisfaction needed to improve or employees would be cut by 40%. Mgrs coached people to higher levels of performance and coached the non-performers out of the org'n. Result: profits increased and needed cuts amounted to only 8%.

Topic	Dysfunctional Pattern of Behavior	Result on Business Outcomes
Making Decisions in a Health Care Org'n managing multiple Medical Centers	- After empowering a committee to develop a new system for improving performance, no process was in place for making decisions to implement the performance improvement system by top management, middle management or by the individual medical centers.	- Five employees spent nine months researching, developing and testing a new performance improvement system within the org'n. Once they could demonstrate measurable results, nobody ofdecision makers was chartered with the role of making the decision to implement the system. **Note:** As a result, over $600,000 was wasted in employee time and in the purchase of the recommended improvement system that was piloted. Some of the wasted money was offset by the success of the pilots., but did not make up for the opportunities lost by the lack of implementation.
Dealing with Conflict in a Division of a Petroleum Company	- When people at the same level are in conflict, it is customary for those involved to ignore one another and bring their issues to upper management for resolution. this took too long and fragmented decisions were made that created new conflicts.	- Based on unresolved conflicts over operational issues between departments, operational systems broke down and production levels were lower than the other divisions within the company. Morale was also negatively impacted by the unresolved disagreements between managers that affected employees. **Note:** After developing the process for resolving conflicts without going to upper management, 55% of all unresolved conflicts were completely resolved within six months. One year later, the same division had the highest levels of production and morale.

Services (information services)—were restructured into each of the five existing plants, which were now business units. To support the team structure, people received training in the value of teamwork and in the skills required of a team-based culture.

When centralized, the organization had relied on two trucks from the maintenance department to serve all five operating plants. With the decentralization, each business unit contained its own maintenance function. But there were still only two trucks. So the business unit managers (all of whom supported and were skilled in the new team structure) met to determine which units would get the trucks and how they could serve the needs of those units who wouldn't get the trucks. They reverted back to their old mindset of "management by control" and their old "habit of behavior" to fight one another, and resulted in an argumentative stalemate that lasted three weeks. Their final decision was that the only way to solve the problem was to purchase three more trucks so that each business unit could have its own truck. Instead of cutting costs, they increased them!

As Stephen Covey pointed out so forcefully in his excellent book, *The Seven Habits of Highly Effective People*, habits can be learned and unlearned, but breaking deeply imbedded habits takes a tremendous effort.[4] The business unit managers were still operating from the old culture of controlling and fighting for resources even though they were the ones who suggested and supported the new team-based organization. The direction was clear, the organization had been restructured, and the technical processes had been re-engineered. But since people continued to operate from their old culture, their sincerest efforts were undermined or sabotaged. Their ultimate "solution" was com-

---

[4] Stephen R. Covey, *The Seven Habits of Highly Effective People,* Simon & Schuster, 1989.

pletely inconsistent with the organization's goal of cutting costs by sharing resources more effectively. It doesn't surprise me that the subject of Covey's latest book is the habits of highly effective families, for families are our fundamental organizational unit. I have found in my work that many principles which are true for organizations, prove true for families as well.

Unfortunately, "patterns of behavior" in an organization are really "habits of behavior" that are hard to break. The conflict over sharing limited resources at the petroleum plant was an automatic behavior based on years of repeated experience that reflected the cultural norms of the organization.

We don't tend to change habits by reading a book, taking a class or developing a new awareness. If it were that easy, people wouldn't have so much trouble losing weight, quitting smoking or reducing alcohol consumption. To change a habit, we must replace the old habit with a new one. It isn't enough to teach people new skills about eating; we must provide them with a system for eating that is repetitive so that over time their new habit of eating takes over automatically.

You may have experienced an organization where the habit for resolving conflict is to talk behind people's backs. When the issue finally reaches the attention of the person targeted, the one who started the rumor denies any involvement. People attend workshops on managing conflict where they practice new communication skills in negotiation and active listening. Also, they may learn people's styles so that they can become more understanding when they are in conflict. However, after the course, they return to the workplace and resume the old habit of behavior. So when a conflict surfaces, they still don't talk. They just become more effective at blaming each other behind each other's backs. If anything, the workshops have enabled them to blame the other person's style more convincingly, using their new communication skills to do so.

Five Steps to Create Organizational Accountability

Developing a culture that gets breakthrough results involves more than changing behaviors or attitudes, or adding new skills to the workforce. It involves developing new patterns and habits of behavior. While it may take years to change all the bad habits of an organization, it requires only about six months to change enough significant habits of behavior to achieve a measurable impact on the organization's desired business outcomes.

Step One: Introduce a New Mindset.

People are familiar with the way things have always been done in the organization. They have no context for understanding the need to change habits of behavior in order to achieve breakthrough results. Therefore, it is essential to present the context for the desired outcomes and goals in terms of the need for survival or the desire to grow. This is accomplished by presenting the Statement of Intention, which will be described in Chapter 5. When people understand the external drivers that affect their organization's viability and survival, along with the mission and values that will address those external drivers, they feel a sense of identity with the organization's desired outcomes.

Unfortunately, most people's mindsets don't change based on awareness alone; they change based on experience. The resulting paradox is that in order for me to change my mindset, I must first experience the results that we are producing. Too often managers wait until the mindset changes before they embark on behavioral changes. This results in stalled efforts. The organization must maintain the focus on outcomes and proceed to implement the new strategy even though not everyone is in agreement or completely understands its purpose.

It can be helpful, though, to provide the organization's history of evolution, describing how previous external drivers have resulted in changes that created the current look and feel of the organization. It's also important to communicate how future changes in external drivers will require the organization to again change its look and feel. This presents a *trend analysis.*

This stage, in which the intention is clarified, is critical for setting up the accountability for achieving results. Without considering the desired outcome, the culture change will seem inconsequential—just another "change for the sake of change"— in order to make people feel good, or to be like the other organizations which are making similar changes.

Step Two: Identify and Reverse Dysfunctional Patterns of Behavior.

The organization needs to identify the "bad" habits of behavior that have kept it from achieving its previous desired outcomes. It also must identify those patterns of behavior that were effective in achieving previous desired outcomes, but that probably won't work to achieve the new desired outcomes. Once identified, it is necessary to develop descriptions of the desired behavior patterns so that people can get a true sense of the new ways of successful functioning in the organization. We refer to these successful ways of functioning as "success factors." One leadership team created a success factor stating: "When you are experiencing conflict with another manager, go to them directly to create a resolution that best meets the needs of the organization as well as the needs of each department represented in the conflict." This was a dramatic change from what had been their habitual behavior of going to upper management to resolve the conflict.

Then the new habits of behavior must be implemented at each level, which will be discussed in Chapter 3. This is one of the most important steps in creating a culture of accountability, since accountability requires linkage among people. This step details the desired expectations for the kinds of linkage necessary for organizational success.

Step Three: Measure the Effectiveness of the New Patterns of Behavior.

It may appear as though the new patterns of behavior aren't working, when in reality people haven't even *tried* them. The organization then spends more time and resources developing another new pattern of behavior, but unfortunately with the same result. This cycle is repeated, creating a sense of "flavor of the month" changes. So the first part of this step is to determine if people are using the new patterns of behavior. The second part is to measure the impact that the new pattern of behavior has on the organization's desired business outcomes. The new behaviors may be successful in terms of implementation, but the results may be counterproductive according to the stated intention and desired business outcomes.

Step Four: Establish Recovery Systems Prior to Implementation.

This is the most important step for ensuring sustained results. There are two natural tendencies that cause organizations to fail.

The first is the tendency to try something new, discover it doesn't work, and then give up, reverting to the old, comfortable way of doing things. The second is to adopt the new habit of behavior, be surprised by a crisis situation and, in crisis mode, revert back to the old habit. As will be discussed in Chapter 3, it is vital that we don't expect perfection. Instead, we must be prepared with a recovery strategy so that we can act when a crisis occurs, when people regress to old habits of behavior, or when we discover that the new behavior isn't working as well as desired. Recovery allows us to continue making progress even when mistakes arise or flaws are discovered.

Step Five: Recognize Results and People.

An accountable organization not only recognizes mistakes, but also recognizes success. It's important to take ownership for success, learn from success and share the learning in order to sustain and expand improvements. Otherwise, while recognition often has the effect of making people feel good, it has a greater purpose in creating an accountable organization: it serves to solidify the new mindset and behaviors that are getting results. This opportunity is missed when organizations fail to provide people with any feedback or recognition regarding actual results before moving on to a new goal. This lack of feedback sends a message to employees that the results achieved weren't important. Why, then, would they want to invest their energy in the next project to improve the organization?

We miss another opportunity when we give recognition to people's efforts without linking their efforts to the results of the change. Then they experience the recognition as empty and meaningless.

Successful recognition involves two steps. The first is recognition of the impact that eliminating dysfunctional habits had on the organization's business outcomes. For instance, we'll feel more valued for our contribution knowing that by resolving the unresolved conflicts we eliminated five inefficient processes that saved us 50 hours of employee time and cost us $20,000 per week in misuse of equipment. Secondly, we must recognize the people's efforts when appropriate and link them to the actual improvements and progress made by the organization. For instance, one organization created a celebration lunch each month to recognize teams that achieved breakthrough results. At the celebration, teams would acknowledge the people (inside and outside of the team) that contributed to achieving the stellar results. Effective recognition reinforces that the elimination of dysfunctional habits and the development of new ones were meaningful.

⊗ **3** ⊗

Break Three "Bad" Habits
of Ineffective Leadership

Myth: Task-oriented leaders who are constantly busy produce successful results.

Truth: Leaders who focus on meaningful priorities and less activity produce successful results.

As the British writer Samuel Johnson noted so astutely in the 18th century, "Nothing will ever be attempted, if all possible objections must be first overcome." The reason so many projects fail is because management tries to perfect the *plan* prior to *implementation*. Often they rationalize their drive for perfection by insisting that they need to ensure buy-in; and argue that people won't buy-in until the plan is perfect. Then, when the organization can't afford to spend more time on the plan, management goes ahead and communicates the implementation strategy, only to run up against resistance and negativity. In an effort to make people comfortable, management decides to study the problem and plan further in order to get less resistance, and the implementation is delayed until the plan is finally deemed to be "perfect." But there will always be resistance. Then, when implementation fails, people who are involved with the implementation (not the planning) are blamed for not achieving the desired results. Management moves to the next goal or project, while employees are still reeling from the current effort. Their resistance to future change strategies and goals is now that much stronger. **We rarely achieve our desired outcomes when the outcomes become a slave to the process.**

The brutality of autocratic and dictatorial leadership that marked much of the first half of this century provoked the development of a series of bad leadership habits that continue to plague organizations and employees to this day. The changes that are required may seem at first glance to herald a return to antiquated, autocratic leadership. But on closer inspection, it will be obvious that accountability-based® leadership not only increases the achievement of business outcomes but also improves employee morale and job satisfaction. The three habits we need to embrace to develop accountable and effective organizations are:

A. Focus on business outcomes rather than on processes

B. Create safety, *not* comfort

C. Become recovery-oriented instead of perfection-oriented.

A. Focus on the Desired Outcome Rather than on the Process

Myth: Perfecting the process creates more successful results.

Truth: Staying focused on the desired outcome achieves successful results.

Dilbert's Wally takes process to new heights of absurdity with something he calls "Process Pride." "It all started when I realized I have no impact on earnings," he explains. "Obviously I can't take pride in the results of my work. But I need pride. Otherwise, how could I maintain my high level of morale? So I learned to take pride in my processes instead of in my results. Everything I do is still pointless, but I'm very proud of the way I do it."

There was a time when it was necessary to be process-oriented. Prior to the Quality Movement, decisions were made autocratically by management without including input from affected employees. This caused frustration and resistance among employees and resulted in inefficient operational systems. The Quality Movement recognized the need for the employees to become directly involved in changing the operational systems for which they were responsible. Unfortunately, employees didn't have the problem solving and decision-making skills required to improve operational systems. Additionally, management had difficulty relinquishing control, which resulted in continued micro-management of the employees. To remedy both of these problems, the Quality Movement emphasized very specific processes aimed at keeping management out of micro-managing, and guiding the employees in effective problem solving and decision-making. By necessity, everyone became process-oriented. This was the most effective way to break the old patterns of autocratic management and dependent employees. Now, thanks to this evolution, we no longer need to be as process-oriented. But it came with a price. Process-driven change efforts lead to three common traps that prevent our change efforts from being responsive.

1. We seek the perfect process and get stuck in analysis paralysis.

   How often have you seen task forces or committees bogged down for months trying in vain to reach consensus? Maybe you've witnessed a group arguing *ad nauseam* over a process issue like: *Do we collect information by doing a survey or by doing interviews?* The truth is, there is no single perfect process; rather, there are many possible routes to the same end. Unless we choose one and start moving towards the goal, we will never arrive. The only way to fail is to fail to move.

2. The desired progress to achieve results comes to a halt because of disagreements regarding the purpose or direction of the goal or project.

   A work unit that becomes polarized due to confusion and disagreement around the purpose of their goal or project gets stuck. As soon as we stop moving towards our outcome, the entire project is at risk. I was once called on to work with a dysfunctional work unit that had been given the charter to improve quality while reducing costs. One part of the unit determined that replacing old, damaged equipment with new equipment would result in greater efficiency and higher customer satisfaction. Another part resisted this solution because it would involve spending money. As a result, no suggestions for improvement came from this work unit for three years. That is when I was called in!

3. We fail to hold people accountable when they are not achieving the outcome.

   Almost everyone knows of chronic non-performers who escape corrective action by blaming the imperfect processes used by the organization. Managers, in turn, think that they need to perfect the processes before they can deal with the non-performer.

Figure 3-1: *As organizations move from Entitlement towards Accountability, they focus more on the outcome than on the process.*

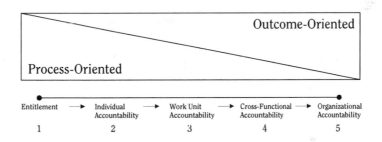

Think back to when you first learned how to drive a car. Do you remember where your focus was? If you're like most people, your eyes focused on the road immediately in front of the car, while your mind focused on the foot action—how much pressure was needed on the gas pedal, the clutch, the brake pedal—and on the activities of your hands on the steering wheel. You were much more alert about the process of driving than you've ever been since. You thought very little about your destination. In fact, your field of vision was limited to perhaps the end of the block. An important part of driver education is to train the driver to focus on the big picture—where you are going—while remaining aware of the process of driving. If you focus exclusively on the process, you are in danger of having an accident. With

---

Stay Focused on the Outcome

For a cable company in the south, survival meant increasing market share. Each department, regardless of function, was given shared responsibility to increase market share. It was determined that costs had to be cut so prices could be more competitive. Also quality service and responsiveness had to improve in order to increase customer satisfaction. Finally, sales efforts had to increase in order to turn non-users into customers. Each department had different and seemingly unrelated functions. Consequently, an analysis was conducted to determine how the specific functions of each department related to market share.

Based on this analysis, each department developed improvement goals designed to increase market share. If a department worked only on meeting it's own self-serving goals, it was held accountable by the management team and redirected to the outcome of increasing market share. Measurements were put into place and tracked weekly to determine the progress made by each department and to uncover obstacles that needed to be removed.

Within six months all of the departments were ahead of schedule on their improvement efforts, and market share and revenue were exceeding their annual target outcome.

---

practice, of course, the process of driving becomes automatic. It is no longer "front of mind."

Similarly, shifting focus back and forth from the current operational environment to the future desired outcome is ideal for leading organizations. If we're driving across the country, we keep checking the map to make sure we're proceeding towards our ultimate destination. If we're behind schedule, we adjust our process by not stopping as often, changing to a less scenic route, or speeding up. When we're not progressing according to plan, we need to examine the process, not for the purpose of perfecting it, but to modify it in order to achieve the desired outcome.

Unfortunately, we tend to lose sight of our destination and get stuck analyzing the process. We can argue endlessly about which fast-food restaurant to stop at on the highway, and lose sight of the fact that we are going to miss our appointment.

B. Create Safety, Not Comfort

Myth: The person who feels comfortable is safe.

Truth: The person who takes action toward his or her desired outcome, despite being uncomfortable, is safe.

Think of the last time that you made a significant paradigm shift in your thinking, attitude or behavior. Did you make this shift when everything was going smoothly in your life or when you were challenged and wondering how (or if) you would get through it? We experience comfort when we are satisfied with our lives. This is not a time when we want to make significant changes. Why rock the boat?

Sometimes, however, although we aren't satisfied with the way things are, we resist new ways of thinking or new behaviors because we are afraid of the consequences. The change might result in the loss of a relationship, the loss of a job, or ridicule. The pain we experience with these kinds of changes feels "punishing."

While we don't choose to modify our behavior when we are comfortable with the way things are, we also don't choose to modify our behavior when we sense that we will be punished for doing so. In order to develop new, effective behaviors, we must feel a sense of "safety" for taking the risks associated with those behaviors. There may be discomfort or even pain involved. But the pain associated with making changes when we feel safe has none of the sense of punishment that is associated with making changes when we do not feel safe. The greater our level of safety, the easier it is for us to change old habits. Generally, our level of safety increases with experience—the more often we have modified old habits, successfully moving through our discomfort in the process, the safer we will feel about making subsequent modifications to our behavior.

Figure 3-2: The three zones of personal transformation

Punishment Zone

Safety Zone

Comfort Zone

A workshop participant illustrated these three zones of personal transformation when she described her process for learning how to ski. Already a beginning skier, she was quite content to remain at that level. However, her friends, all more advanced skiers, wanted her to ski with them. Nervously, she agreed to try an intermediate slope. Although frightened, she decided she could go down the hill as long as she allowed herself to fall. Twelve falls later she was down the hill in one piece and decided to try it again. This time she made it down with only five falls. If she had stayed comfortable, she would still have been stuck on the "bunny slopes" and would have felt unsafe as an intermediate skier. If her friends had taken her to one of the advanced slopes, she could have been seriously hurt. Her level of fear in that case would have felt punishing. As it was, she worked through the discomfort she felt, took the risk and increased her safety in skiing.

Figure 3-3: *As a person's safety zone increases, they more easily adapt*
to change.

A Person Unsafe with Change.	A Person Safe with Change.
	Punishment Zone
Punishment Zone	Safety Zone
Safety Zone	Comfort Zone
Comfort Zone	

Some people have been in the same job for thirty years, had the same co-workers for twenty years and the same supervisor for fifteen years. Their comfort has been firmly established by the stability of the environment. When a restructuring is announced, they automatically feel punished by the prospect of change. They are not accustomed to changes in their working conditions.

Figure 3-4: *As organizations move from Entitlement to Accountability,*
comfort decreases and safety increases.

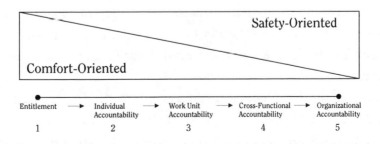

The Demise of the Comfortable Organization

Management generally wants to create a safe environment for employees. This, of course, is appropriate when it relates to the physical environment. And, while it is also appropriate for the cultural environment, the mistake most managers make is to equate "safety" with "comfort." Instead of creating an environment in which it is safe to take risks, managers create an environment where being comfortable is the goal. However, "real" safety occurs when employees can take real chances and know they will be supported.

Organizations with high levels of comfort rather than safety are generally polite organizations where people don't challenge one another and where conflict is avoided. Decisions are put on hold until it is too late to make a good decision or until crisis takes over. Planning is preferred to taking action, since more risk is involved in taking action. Projects are delayed over and over again, because no one is willing to admit stumbling blocks or obstacles. Moreover, organizations that emphasize comfort also tend to be the most political, making decisions and creating policies based on influence rather than on the need to achieve specific outcomes.

The "comfortable" environment promoted by management is ideally suited for the non-performers who are never coached and who are transferred to other managers as a "sweeping under the carpet" solution. We know the environment is comfortable when new solutions, projects or change efforts are put on hold because people are resisting even though the organization's survival is at risk.

Emphasizing comfort can be very costly to the organization and result in even greater pain and punishment to the employees. About 20 years ago in a major California university, a team of typists was ordered by management to take classes in word processing and the computer. The typists resisted the transition to new technology, explaining that they had always used typewriters and that typewriters worked just fine. Management wanted to make them comfortable on the job, so they reversed their decision to require the training. Within five years, the entire department was let go because the people lacked the skills to perform the clerical jobs now demanded by their customers. This was a heavy price to pay for being comfortable. Learning, changing and growing all require that we experience the discomfort associated with taking the risks to move into uncharted waters.

Organizations can't allow people's natural resistance to change to cause the process of transformation to be stopped. Nor is this the time to "empower" them to confront their bad habits or antiquated methods by themselves; doing so will only make them feel alone and abandoned. Managers must provide guidance and encouragement to move people through their discomfort, whether expressed as resistance, apathy, hurt or rebellion.

C. Focus on Recovery, Not on Perfection

> **Myth:** Being perfection-oriented optimizes performance
>
> **Truth:** Being recovery-oriented optimizes performance.

Focusing on perfection is one of the great diseases of modern organizations. We plan until the plan is perfect, we don't make decisions until we are sure that the decision is the "right" one to

Speedy Recovery at a Medical Center

A Medical Center needed to consolidate two floors in order to reduce costs and provide better health care to patients. Management directed the change that was planned by a committee consisting of people on each of the two units being moved. When the plan was implemented, both units worked well together to make the necessary changes. Both had recovery plans in place to deal with the little problems that would take place during the transition.

However, one of the units was beginning to see some major breakdowns that no one had anticipated in the planning stages. Instead of responding with negativity, complaints and resistance, they presented top management with data demonstrating the problem. As part of the recovery plan for implementation, management was able to evaluate the data, make a decision to move the unit back to its original floor, and begin to work on a new implementation plan. The goals of the implementation weren't completely lost. In fact, even though the unit went back to the original floor temporarily, the nursing staff integrated the desired outcomes for the consolidation into their functioning. The amazing part of their recovery process was that it all took place within a period of two weeks, and **resulted in increased morale and improved customer service to patients.**

make, and we end up in analysis paralysis, unable to create the perfect solution. We talk about creating a learning environment, or an environment of continuous improvement, yet in our demand for perfection we eliminate the safety to make mistakes, to take risks and to break away from the status quo. We operate with the illusion that once a plan is in place, a decision is made, or a solution is implemented, it can't be adjusted. And we worry that we'll be blamed when it is discovered that our plan, decision or solution isn't perfect.

While there are some aspects of planning and decision-making that can't be adjusted, like the purchasing of major equipment or the building of a new office structure, most plans and decisions must be modified upon implementation. Diane Dreher discusses this in her book, *The Tao of Personal Leadership*, where she notes, "Tao leaders have the strength of bamboo—able to bend, blend with circumstances, adjust to change and overcome adversity. They can meet any challenge with courage and compassion."[1]

The problem is that when we expect perfection, we don't plan for imperfection. We are then unprepared when the unexpected takes place. This results in the sort of crisis that causes breakdown.

Some managers fear that creating recovery systems upfront offers an excuse for not performing. However, for most top performing groups outside the business environment, recovery systems are a way of life. Indeed, they are a direct means for achieving high performance.

Consider a World Series baseball team, a nationally known theater company or a military operation. Each one desires perfect performance, but their route to perfection is not only through practicing for perfection, but also through the development of "recovery" systems in case of human error or unexpected incidents. Baseball teams practice their recovery play when someone drops the ball. Theater companies practice their recovery system when someone forgets his or her lines or when a part of the set malfunctions. Military units develop contingency plans.

In organizations, however, we expect perfection and then blame either the person or the process when breakdown occurs. While everyone is busy blaming each other, the desired business outcome is missed, resulting in yet another failure. Worst of all, people tend to give up, feeling that no amount of time or effort

---

[1] Diane Dreher, *The Tao of Personal Leadership,* Harper & Row, 1996.

will ever be sufficient to allow for a successful implementation of change.

Creating a recovery system is a way to stay in the game rather than forfeiting the game altogether. Mistakes will occur and unexpected events will take place, but for the organization that has a recovery system in place, adjustments can be made swiftly and effectively to achieve the desired outcomes. There are three different situations in which recovery systems can be applied. First, recovery is critical for **strategic planning efforts.** Many organizations recognize the need for scenario planning or contingency planning in today's changing environment. They create different scenarios based on the variables of external drivers and performance results that could take place.

Second, recovery is essential for **project planning**. As a result of unforeseen circumstances or unresolved problems, projects can be seriously delayed. Usually, project managers feel a sense of ownership for the project. They don't want to feel a sense of failure. Consequently, neither the mechanism nor the safety exists to surface serious problems that arise. So no opportunity exists for others to help create alternative solutions. A decision can't be made to modify or even to abort the project.

Figure 3-5: As organizations move from Entitlement to Accountability, they become less perfection-oriented and more recovery-oriented.

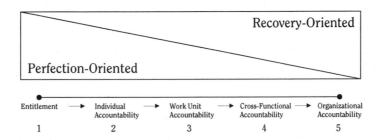

Entitlement →	Individual Accountability	→ Work Unit Accountability	→ Cross-Functional Accountability	→ Organizational Accountability
1	2	3	4	5

Such a situation occurred at one of the largest financial institutions in Canada, where the improvement of computer technology used throughout the organization was a major priority. Millions of dollars were spent on a project to develop new software and hardware systems. The project was delayed for months, but the delays were not brought to the attention of upper management until it was too late: the delays had reached crisis proportions. After several months and millions of dollars of investment, the project had to be completely aborted. Even though team members had been concerned about the delays, there was no safety and no recovery systems were in place to raise the possibility of project failure until millions of dollars had already been spent. A recovery system provides the safety and mechanism to surface and address serious problems.

Third, recovery systems are essential for the **improvement of relationships in the workplace**. As organizations become more accountable, they tend to develop agreements among departments, functions, levels and team members. It is critical that recovery systems are in place so that if agreements are broken, the people involved have a mechanism for discussing and amending them. Otherwise, their anger about the broken agreement may cause them to abandon the agreements completely.

Recovery systems are the key to creating an environment of safety that leads to greater accountability. We can solve only those problems that we know about. Without an effective recovery system, problems remain hidden, conflicts remain unresolved, and the resulting culture of non-performance continues as the norm within the organization. There is no excuse for failing to improve current processes and functioning when a recovery system is in place. Problems surface in a timely manner before they become a major crisis, and everyone enjoys a sense of satisfaction in overcoming the natural challenges that show up in the workplace.

☜ **4** ☞

The Formula
to Achieve Breakthroughs

Myth: Empowering people helps them to overcome their fear of change.

Truth: Guiding people to action helps them to move through their fear of change.

Before people can be more accountable and take action to pursue a new direction, they must have a sense that, like the beginning skier, they are safe enough to risk action that catapults them out of their comfort zone. Otherwise, taking action on a new direction will feel punishing. Paradoxically, however, *the only way for them to increase their level of safety is for them to be accountable and to take action*. As our safety increases through taking action, so does our comfort. The skier's comfort increased when she became an intermediate level skier.

My daughter went through a similar process at the age of eight when she asked me to teach her how to dive at our local pool. We stood at the side of the pool and I showed her the position for going into the water head-first. She moved into position, stood there for a few moments, then straightened up again. "Dad," she said, "you dive first to show me what it looks like."

I gladly performed a dive for her. Climbing out of the pool, I said, "Now it's your turn."

She got into position, then quickly straightened up again. "I'm confused," she said. "Please show me another time."

I realized she was up against her fear. At this point, I could try to make my daughter feel more comfortable by continuing to dive for her, but I knew that the only way for her to feel safe diving was for her to take the action herself. I urged her to get back into position and just give it a try. I reassured her that I would stand right there to make sure she was okay.

She gathered up her courage and dove, landing with a splat as she performed her first belly flop. She knew it wasn't the perfect dive, but now she had created the safety to try it again until she could improve her dive to her satisfaction. Safety to take risks leads to taking action and being accountable. By taking action, we create a new level of safety for ourselves that leads to bigger challenges and change as illustrated in the following figures.

Figure 4-1: Safety leads to Accountability which promotes greater Safety

Figure 4-2: Moving to Denial promotes greater Pain

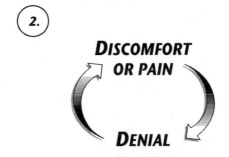

Being safe to take risks does not mean that we feel no pain or discomfort. On the contrary, the Safety Zone always involves a degree of discomfort. But instead of fleeing from that discomfort, we face it, armed with the knowledge that action provides the antidote. The skier taking action and skiing down the hill relieved the discomfort she felt at the prospect of skiing down an intermediate hill. My daughter's fear of diving was relieved by the act of diving.

As illustrated in Figure 4-2, to deny the discomfort only makes it worse. When we take an aspirin to relieve a headache

Denial at Work

A team of project managers was several months late completing their project. They asked me to review their process in order to find the hidden breakdown causing their problem. I asked how their meetings were going. "Our team meetings are great!" claimed the team leader. "We have an agenda, everyone shows up on time, well prepared for the discussion. We're clear on the outcomes and everyone participates, sharing ideas openly."

I offered to review their process at the next meeting. Sure enough, the leader was correct on every account. I was most impressed with their openness in discussing the issues that surfaced. However, about a quarter of the way through the meeting it became clear that they weren't making any decisions or taking any action. I stopped the group and expressed my observation, but they insisted that they needed to have this discussion before they could make any decisions.

Half the meeting went by. I repeated my observation. "No outcomes have been accomplished yet," I said. They insisted that they were on track with regard to their agenda. Finally, at the end of the meeting I asked the team how they felt about their meeting. "It was a great meeting!" they told me. "We had a great discussion!"

Not only were they in denial, they were slaves to the process of their "perfect meeting." I agreed that they had held a great discussion. But I also reflected the other truth of the situation, which was that they *had made no progress on their desired outcomes for the meeting* and would need to have the same discussion again at their next meeting.

Aware that they might perceive me as being judgmental, I asked a question to help surface the truth of the situation more clearly. "How often do you have great discussions, but then have to deal with the same issues at the next meeting?" "Most of the time," they admitted. "No wonder you are late on your project," I said. "You aren't making decisions or taking the actions necessary for making progress." This left them stunned, feeling the full force of the pain of their denial.

Now they were ready to face their need to change. I told them I had also observed that they had the thinking ability and skills necessary to solve their issues. Reassuring though this may have been, I knew that it did not provide them with enough safety to lead them to action. When people are experiencing the discomfort of the situation, they are often discouraged, confused and consumed with self-doubt.

Now that they were receptive, I spent the next hour leading them through the process of surfacing issues, making decisions, and agreeing to take action. Based on this demonstration, they were now empowered to carry the process forward to future meetings. As a result, they completed their project in six months, one month ahead of schedule.

from on the job stress, we generally also go into denial about the stress. Of course, although the headache might go away temporarily, unless the underlying stress vanishes as well, we'll probably end up with stronger headaches down the road. So we take extra-strength aspirin to dull the pain and discomfort. The cycle will continue until the pain grows intolerable. When the body experiences too much pain it goes into shock, but when our emotions experience too much pain we go numb. So we no longer feel the stress of the job until we go on vacation and discover, five days later, what we're really like when we aren't stressed.

In a workplace of constant change and pressure to achieve greater results, people tend to respond either with discomfort and pain, or numbness and denial. And just think: *These are people who have been "empowered" to lead during the last ten years*! The question now becomes, how do we lead people to greater levels of safety and accountability, so they will be truly empowered to assume the risks of breaking old paradigms?

Having the Courage to Tell the Truth

If a non-performer on your team thinks that he is doing a good job, and no one tells him differently, does his performance change? Of course not. Therefore, when someone is in denial, it is important to hold him accountable by reflecting to him **the truth of the situation.** This truth is not a philosophical truth, but a simple, accurate and nonjudgmental reflection of the events that are taking place. Any hint of judgment will send that person into a defensive posture, and he'll return to his state of denial.

We tend to withhold telling the truth because we are afraid of the reaction we may get. The person may feel angry or hurt by our feedback. In order for us to remain comfortable, we "dance" around the truth in a way that makes our message unclear. Even worse, we don't share the "truth" with the person who is the subject of the comment; we share it with others who will agree with us. Jack Stack summarized this point well in his book, *The Great Game of Business*, when he said, "...you only build credibility by telling the truth. You simply can't operate unless people believe you and believe one another."[1]

Of course, whenever we are telling the "truth", it is still only our perception that we are revealing, which is why it is important to refrain from our judgments and opinions as much as possible. It is especially important to refrain from telling the "truth" as a self-righteous position.

Figure 4-3: Pain is the passageway between Denial and Safety

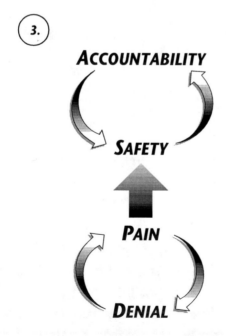

---

[1] Jack Stack, *The Great Game of Business*, Currency Doubleday, 1991.

Figure 4-4: Reflect the "TRUTH" of the situation.

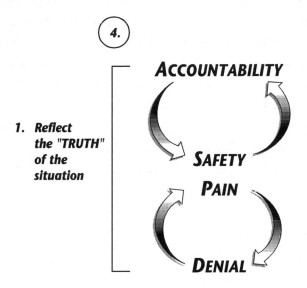

Figure 4-5: Offer Acceptance, Belief and Encouragement

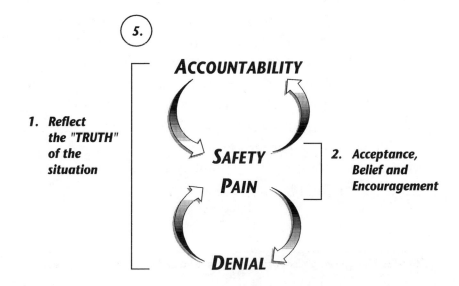

Don't Remove People's Pain

When people accept the truth relating to their denial, they will feel a level of pain or discomfort. This is not bad news. We often experience our greatest transformations when we are feeling uncomfortable as a result of our current situation. Charles Handy describes this stage of "pain" in his section on the "Sigmoid Curve." In essence, every curve goes up and then down. He says, "The secret to constant growth is to start a new curve before the first one peters out."[2] However, when we are moving from one curve to another or one state to another, it is a time of confusion, frustration and discontent until we see the new path more clearly.

When people are feeling the "pain" of the truth and the current situation, they may express their pain in many forms including anger, resistance, hurt, rebellion or apathy. We must remember that their expression isn't wrong, in need of correction, or a problem to be solved. Holding people accountable when they are in pain or making them comfortable by taking away pain only leads them back into denial. Instead, we must provide them with enough safety to permit them to feel (rather than deny) their pain. We do this by recognizing that they are uncomfortable or in pain about the situation and then by expressing our belief in them to be successful. I am grateful for the mentors in my life who believed in me when I stopped believing in myself during periods of confusion and self-doubt. It is also important to encourage the person to keep moving and progressing, since it is only through our movement and action that we can transition past our fear of the unknown.

---

[2] Charles Handy, *The Age of Paradox*, Harvard Business School Press, 1994.

Stop "Empowering" and Start Guiding

One of the greatest errors of the last decade is the notion of empowering people whenever we want them to take action. Under the guise of empowerment, managers abdicate their role as providers of leadership and guidance. This creates great frustration and discouragement among employees.

When people are experiencing the discomfort of change, we need to provide specific action steps that will guide them through their pain to the point at which they can take action and achieve results. When my daughter was standing at the side of the pool, it wouldn't have worked for me to empower her. I needed to encourage and direct her into the water so she could gain her own experience and create her own safety to try it again.

Figure 4-6: Provide Guidance and Specific Action Steps

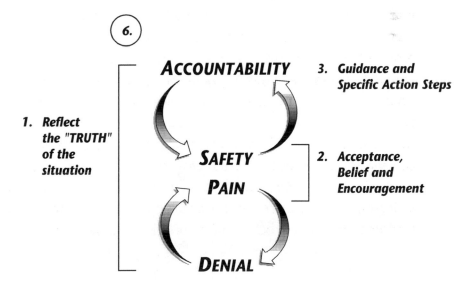

The following pattern is sadly familiar to many of us. Management reflects the truth of the situation and announces a change. People respond with resistance. Recognizing people's discomfort, management revises their story of the truth so they can slow down or stop the change. But eventually the change can no longer be avoided. Then management forces the change on people by "empowering" them to make the changes on their own (or else face serious consequences). Now people feel completely abandoned by management. They decide that management has no credibility, and take on a cynical perspective in order to avoid further disappointment.

This is what happened at a major communications company in California which announced one September that 30% of a 500-person department was going to be downsized in three months. I was called in to help the management team (which was also going to be cut 30%) develop a strategy for restructuring the process. Not surprisingly, people were expressing plenty of grief. Once we moved past the anger, we created an implementation plan to which everyone agreed. The team made progress on the plan for eight weeks, at which point I went back for a follow-up session. People entered the room even angrier than before. I couldn't understand why, since I knew that they had made steady progress on their plan. It turned out that management had reversed the decision to perform the downsizing, claiming that they had acted too hastily. However, management also said that this wouldn't prevent them from downsizing the following year.

It is critical for managers and employees alike to start reflecting the truth, providing encouragement when others are feeling overwhelmed and doubtful, and more importantly, providing guidance in the form of specific action to move through the change.

Ten Ways to Create *Safe* Accountability in Your Organization

1. Set clear and mutually agreed-upon expectations with people with regard to both performance and behavior. This reduces confusion, mixed messages, and judgments of non-performance.

2. Share information openly and timely to avoid unnecessary surprises.

3. Surface any conflict directly with the person involved. Focus on ways to avoid conflict in the future. (This is far more effective than avoiding the person, telling everyone else about the conflict, or blaming the person as the one who was wrong.)

4. Provide encouragement, guidance and other forms of support to individuals who need to make a change but who may not realize the importance, or the process, of doing so. Typically, we either ignore people struggling because we're too busy, or we sympathize with their discomfort and let them off the hook.

5. Focus on functional roles and processes, rather than position and power, to accomplish outcomes.

6. Support the development of people and systems in order to respond to the needs of tomorrow and to avoid reacting only to crises.

7. Monitor and measure the results of each team and individual so that people know exactly where they stand. This is the only way to make people aware of their successes and their need for improvement.

8. Do not allow people to perform poorly without making it clear that their performance is unacceptable. Skirting the issue only causes people to feel deceived and victimized. No one benefits by carrying a poor performer. The organization loses, and so does the individual.

9. Follow up on commitments so that people can depend on your words and your consistency. If you are unable to keep a commitment, let people know as soon as you know.

10. Let others know the care, appreciation and compassion you feel, instead of holding back. Honor their humanity as well as your own. When all is said and done, we are FIRST human beings with fears, needs and imperfections, and SECOND, employees hired to complete a job.

∞ **5** ∞

Leadership Roles
that Produce Breakthrough Results

Myth: Senior management must act accountable
before the organization can be
accountable.

Truth: Middle management must act accountable
as a unified team before the organization
can be accountable.

I grew up believing that teachers taught and students learned. The roles were clear and leadership was a singular role held by the teacher. While this approach to education was changing by the time I became a teacher, it was still clear that my responsibility was to lead the educational experience for students. One year I taught a high school general math class comprised of 16 and 17 year olds who had difficulty with simple arithmetic. Adding, subtracting, multiplying and dividing were painful processes for these students even though they were old enough to drive and were approaching voting age.

Peggy, a particularly cooperative student in the class, began to experience some breakthroughs in completing the math assignments, so I introduced her to basic algebra. She understood the concepts, could complete the homework assignments and was progressing well. Then an incident occurred which changed my perspective about teaching forever.

I was working with a group of students who were having difficulty adding and subtracting fractions when another student let me know he was ready to progress to his next level of math equations. John was doing well, and I didn't have time to work with him in that moment, so I asked Peggy to show him the math calculations she was working on. Later, when I had a break, I checked to see how John was getting along. To my surprise, he was doing far better than I would have expected. Peggy had turned out to be an excellent teacher. I continued this model of "chain teaching" as students progressed to the higher levels of math problems. By the end of the year, nine students were doing algebra. All had taught someone else at some point through this process of students as teachers. Until then, students in a general math class had been categorized as unable to handle algebra. Now they were not only able to learn algebra, they were also teaching it!

A similar strategy can be used in the work place. Organizations include people at both management and non-management levels. Typically, we assume that leadership is the exclusive domain of management. Yet successful organizations have leaders at all levels of the organization. While each person's leadership role is different, it is critical to have leaders who will direct people toward a unified focus, implement changes to achieve the impossible, develop others in the organization, and bring new skills and expertise to the organization. Regardless of whether people are in management or non-management positions, there will be leadership roles for them.

When an organization isn't accomplishing its desired outcomes, the tendency is for employees to blame supervisors, for middle managers to blame upper managers, and for upper managers to blame employees. When people are blaming each other for the problems that exist in an organization, it is a sign that they are not assuming leadership for solving those problems. The notion that leadership is reserved for people in management denies the responsibility which each person has to take charge of and be accountable for his or her performance and relationship with others. When an organization is committed to accountability, leadership roles exist at all levels. People are accountable for moving themselves, their team, and their organization to the next level of performance within the parameters of their respective roles within the organization. Confusion regarding the roles appropriate to the different levels in an organization contributes to the "blame game" and to a general lack of accountability.

We can determine the roles for each level within the organization by examining the "direct" accountability required both in achieving results and in linking with other levels or functions within the organization. Accordingly, executives assume the role of **catalysts for achieving results,** middle managers the role of **change agents,** and employees the role of **customer activists.**

Stop Waiting for Executives to Change

Executives are directly accountable for the current overall performance of the organization in terms of profitability and customer satisfaction, as well as for the organization's future viability. None of these responsibilities, however, are within the executives' direct control. Executives like to *think* they're in control, but in their hearts rests the frightening awareness that they're the only ones in the organization who are *not* in control. While executives can make overreaching decisions to cut costs in order to achieve greater profitability, they are not in control of the direct performance that impacts the customer. Nor are they fortune-tellers who can predict the future viability of the organization based on all of the variables of the external drivers affecting the organization. At best, they can make educated guesses.

When we don't have control over our areas of responsibility, we feel highly vulnerable. As a result, executives create as much safety as they can for themselves. This may explain some of the actions (or, more correctly, *inactions*) for which they are often criticized. Have you ever seen a proposed recommendation postponed on an executive agenda meeting after meeting? When was the last time you received direction or a mission statement from executives that clearly communicated specific expectations that the organization could be held accountable for achieving? Have you ever wondered why your organization decides to implement a popular improvement program adopted by other, similar organizations even though it didn't seem to make sense for your organization? All of these situations have one thing in common: they are all ways of maintaining a level of safety and avoiding direct accountability—especially accountability that is readily apparent to the rest of the organization. No wonder executives will micro-manage situations that seem to be getting out of control—doing so allows them to claim at least a modicum of control over the organization's performance.

After witnessing similar behaviors of executives in various industries and countries, I have concluded that the dynamics of accountability and safety have more to do with their behavior than with their ineffectiveness as leaders. In fact, executives are generally very skilled at keeping the different factions happy by maintaining a high level of safety for all involved parties including the board, the shareholders, management, employees and the public. Each group has its own needs and agenda, which must be carefully balanced by executives. The executive's challenge is to be accountable for effectively satisfying each of these customers. So, instead of blaming executives for not performing their role in the way we think is most appropriate, we need to promote a role for executives that both protects their need for safety and contributes to the organization's accountability for achieving its desired business outcomes.

Executives are *Catalysts for Achieving Results,* Not *Change Agents*

A CEO of a national journal was faced with a declining market. Besides having to create a new look for his publication, he had to change the focus of its content in order to appeal to a wider audience. At staff meetings, employees would grumble about the journal's lack of direction. "We should be focused more on the environment," claimed one employee. "I think spirituality should be our major purpose," said another. Someone else claimed that the journal should stick to its roots and continue running articles on traditional research from leading studies on psychology.

They all expressed their views with much conviction, and these views reflected their own interests and those of their colleagues who had similar interests. However, none of the staff were accountable for the results of their opinions in terms of ensuring customer acceptance and profitability. The organization remained fragmented for several months while staff members continued to present their opinions at meetings on this subject. At last the CEO took a different approach to determining the journal's direction.

The CEO determined the "ideal" customer base by age and interest in order to provide the largest readership possible. Then he had a market research company survey those readers for their specific interests and issues. The acquired information provided the basis for a clear direction of focus for the journal. Based on customer interests, the CEO clearly explained the new direction of the journal and was able to win support from most of the staff, even though most of them had earlier made very different suggestions. Within a few weeks, the organization demonstrated unity, focus and alignment, and readership improved within the next several months.

Like many people, I was conditioned to think that change had to begin with top management. This translated to the expectation that executives had to change before anyone else could. While I have seen some executive teams become very accountable, very few have sufficiently adopted the very changes which they promoted. Other managers and employees then use this as an excuse to resist becoming more accountable. After working with many different organizations in different industries, I am convinced that it is *not* necessary for executives to first model the level of accountability they are promoting before the rest of the organization can become more accountable. *Executives are not the change agents.*

Executives are the *catalysts for achieving results* and setting the tone for the culture. As such, their role is to articulate the direction and desired outcomes in a clear and unified front to establish the path for movement and progress. If executives aren't clear about the desired outcomes and priorities, then the organization will become paralyzed in confusion. Their communication must be strategically delivered to create the greatest level of focus and action, as detailed in Chapter 7.

Executives: Stop Hiding and Take a Stand

One of the most frequent complaints I hear throughout an organization concerns "lack of direction." Mission statements full of rhetoric, "flavor of the month" change efforts, and a multitude of (often-conflicting) priorities bombard people. Without clear direction, managers can't effectively prioritize workloads or make good decisions, and paralysis results. Executives must stop avoiding their true accountability and take a stand on the future direction of the organization.

The future direction is determined by the "external drivers" to which the organization must respond. These are conditions that the organization can't change, and therefore, must respond to in order to stay viable. I refer to external drivers as "non-negotiables." They include factors such as:

- Changes in Customer Expectations
- Technology Advancements
- Societal Needs
- Competitive Trends
- Government Regulation and Intervention
- Trends in Supplier Markets
- Financial Constraints
- Market Trends

Executives have more direct access to the organization's external drivers than anyone else in the organization. Since they aren't managing daily operations, they can serve on government committees that impact legislation affecting the organization. They can participate in community groups that represent the societal trends in the customer base (as opposed to the needs of individual customers which are best represented by employees). And they can analyze the other external drivers that impact the organization, including market studies, economic changes, financial trends, technological advances, and so on. While all other levels of the organization are responsible for ensuring the daily performance that serves current customers, executives have access to the external drivers that continue to prepare and shape the organization for the future.

Therefore, the primary responsibility of executives is to establish a clear direction for the future of the organization as well as clear financial, cultural, operational and related boundaries for creating the future. While they may gather input from others, it is not acceptable for executives to delegate the decision of the organization's direction to a committee. Ultimately, they are the ones responsible for producing a strategic business plan that clearly articulates the necessary business outcomes required for the organization to thrive over the next few years. It is also their responsibility to identify the type of culture necessary for achieving those business outcomes in the most effective manner. Identifying the ideal culture is not just a question of ethics or values, but also one of performance execution to achieve business outcomes. At the heart of this direction is the determination of whether the organization will function at a level 2, 3 or 4 on the Accountability Continuum (individual, work-unit or cross-functional).

Part of this role includes communicating a clear message about the desired outcome and priorities, as well as providing the understanding, background and context for necessary changes. As will be described in Chapter 6, this includes creating an "Intention" about the future: a detailed vision that consists of the mission for the organization, the values representing the culture of the organization, and the response to those external drivers which direct the organization's future.

The desired business outcomes and direction of the organization may evolve in a fast paced and changing business environment, which is why executives must be accountable for setting *priorities* with regard to them. With continuous changes being forged by the external drivers, executives must update and clarify the priorities on a regular basis. Otherwise, people continue to add to their list of priorities, and they become fragmented and overwhelmed. As a result, they fail to achieve the expected business results necessary to make progress. All executives must continually restate the desired outcomes and articulate the priorities of the organization as the emphasis shifts.

Because executives are responsible for the direction of the organization, they are also accountable for ensuring that the organization stays on track. While they aren't responsible for taking specific actions, they are responsible for monitoring the progress made to achieve the organization's priorities and direction. This includes both performance-oriented priorities as well as cultural changes directly associated with achieving the organization's desired business outcomes.

Executives are also accountable for identifying and communicating the consequences of failing to achieve the organization's desired business outcomes. These must be presented not as a threat of punishment, but as an honest reflection of the reality of the impact such failures will have on the organization's viability.

Finally, executives must guide and coach middle managers on their strategy of operational change based on the desired business outcomes. This does not mean that executives are expected to *solve* tactical operational problems; only that they must guide the strategy for overcoming global organizational challenges that prevent progress. For example, this may involve finding ways to use the organization's resources more effectively by setting up cross-functional operation systems. Finally, executives need to ensure that the linkages and functioning between all levels of the organization are maintained properly by middle managers.

The Plight of Middle Management

Danny, one of my closest childhood friends, was the first born in a family of three children. As the oldest, Danny was clearly the leader of his younger sister and brother. Since I was an only child, I was interested in observing him and his siblings interact. One day Danny's parents asked him to take care of his younger brother and sister while they went out to buy groceries for dinner. "Don't let them get into any trouble while we're gone," said his dad.

Danny did his best to live up to his parents' expectations. At the same time, he also wanted to play with his brother and sister. Of course, as soon as he took on the role as protector and leader, his siblings banded together, leaving him out. Soon a fight broke out between the two younger children. Danny stepped in as the boss, which only fueled the fight since his brother and sister were not about to cooperate with his new authority. By the time his parents returned we were all yelling and screaming at each other.

Danny's father turned to him, furious. "What happened?" he demanded. "Can't we leave you in charge for even a half-hour without World War III breaking out!??" Danny was sent to his room, I was sent home, and Danny's brother and sister were sent outside to play.

When I talk with middle managers and supervisors, they make me think of Danny. They're caught in the middle, desperately trying to serve executives who "don't understand," while the employees are fighting among themselves, not cooperating, and blaming middle management for the problems.

Because executives are not directly involved with day-to-day operations, they are not well positioned to control operational improvements. Middle management, on the other hand, is ideally positioned to do so. Executives who insist on being the ones to control operational processes end up becoming roadblocks. In such circumstances, middle managers and employees will make recommendations for improvement, and these will go to the executive team for approval where they will sit for months waiting for executives to make a decision. The reality is that while executives can make decisions as to the global direction of the organization, they are too far removed to make decisions regarding the day-to-day operations. But unfortunately, many executive teams are afraid to hand over that control to the middle managers.

Actually, there is good reason for their reluctance since many companies are set up such that middle managers are accountable for their own department, as if it were an isolated island within the organization. Some call these departments "silos." While virtually every department has a major impact on the success of every other department, conflicting priorities and the desire to make one's own department look best then creates the territorialism that dominates most organizations. Middle managers feel disempowered, since as individuals they don't have the authority to make meaningful decisions that will impact the way the organization functions. This creates the barriers most bitterly discussed among employees.

Ironically, middle managers are positioned to serve as the ideal cross-functional team in the organization, since they represent the operations of every major department. While their job should be to make the operational decisions as a cross-functional team that will lead the organization to achieving its desired business outcomes, they instead generally get bogged down in territorial in-fighting over position, power, and resources. As a result, the improvements recommended by middle managers tend to be shortsighted at best, causing middle managers to lose the respect of both executives and employees. Over time, they become caretakers rather than initiators of improvement.

For an organization to optimize its performance and to quickly respond to the demands of its customers and external environment, the role of middle management must change. Middle managers must become accountable not only for their own department but also for the operational effectiveness of the entire organization. Janet Lowe presents the views of Jack Welch in her book *Jack Welch Speaks*, where Jack Welch is quoted as saying, "Boundaryless behavior laughs at the concept of little kingdoms called finance, engineering, manufacturing and marketing, sending each other specs and memos, and instead gets them all together in a room to wrestle with issues as a team."[1] The reality described here demands an entirely different mindset as to the structure and role of middle management.

---

[1] Janet Lowe, *Jack Welch Speaks: Wisdom from the World's Greatest Business Leader,* John Wiley & Sons, Inc. 1998.

Middle Managers: From Territorial Tycoons to a Team of Change Agents

Revolutionaries in history attacked the "establishment" on the basis of a "cause." In the United States, the English "Red Coats" represented the "establishment" and the "cause" was democracy. In organizations, the "establishment" is represented by antiquated methods of leadership along with dysfunctional operational habits. The "cause" is achieving *breakthrough results in half the time expected*. The Revolutionaries are middle managers dedicated as a team of "Change Agents" to eliminate dysfunctional processes and habits that undermine successful achievement of desired outcomes.

While a Strategic Business Plan developed by executives outlines the specific direction of the organization, a Strategic Operations Plan is what translates that direction into action. Therefore, middle managers, as the ones overseeing and controlling operations, are in the best position to develop and manage an organization's Strategic Operations Plan. This can be accomplished only when each manager has a full understanding of the impact that each department has on the other departments. The operational strategy, utilization of resources, and priorities must be linked and integrated in order to ensure a unified, coordinated and aligned focus and effort. Otherwise, operational fragmentation pulls apart the organization and causes it to spin its wheels.

To achieve this level of effectiveness, middle managers must be formed into a cross-functional team where they develop a clear intention of leadership for which they all become accountable. This intention of leadership should include their commitment to ensuring the operational success of the organization as a higher priority than the success of their own individual department. Tom Peters describes this well in his book, *Thriving on Chaos,* where he notes that "...Middle managers are to be responsible for seeking out and battering down the very functional barriers that they were formerly paid to protect. They are to be charged with making things happen, come hell or high water."[2]

The intention of leadership is always futuristic and, as such, it involves a "stretch" of the current situation. Specifically, it includes a description of the reputation the leaders want to have with employees, a description of the teamwork necessary to achieve this reputation, and a description of their role in ensuring organizational viability and success. All of these dimensions are included in the statement of intention developed by the leadership team at St. Charles Medical Center, which is looked at in Chapter 6.

Grounded in this commitment and in the practice of sharing information and resources, middle management develops a Strategic Operational Plan that will ensure that their Strategic Business Plan will be achieved within the financial constraints set forth by senior management. As a team, middle managers identify the priorities of the operation. They identify the dysfunctional habits that require change, the strategy for making those changes, and the tracking to ensure transformation of the culture. This includes aspects of the organization's functioning as demonstrated by performance management systems, strategic communication systems, recognition systems, decision-making processes, and processes for resolving conflicts. Middle management functions as a team that: a) makes operational decisions with global and cross-functional ramifications; b) takes action by developing new habits to replace dysfunctional

---

[2] Tom Peters, *Thriving on Chaos: Handbook for a Management Revolution,* Harper Perennial, 1987.

ones; and c) resolves conflicts or problems that block employee success.

In an accountable organization, middle managers also become accountable to one another. Each department performs in accordance with an agreed upon operational strategic plan which is created and monitored by the middle management team.

The role of middle management, then, becomes two-fold:

1. Middle managers are responsible for the global operations of the organization, the culture that ensures effective functioning and linkage between departments, and the monitoring of organizational performance to ensure that business outcomes are being achieved.

2. Middle managers are responsible for the performance of their respective departments and for eliminating dysfunctional habits in their department that prevents departmental and organizational success.

Individual Accountability—
The Heart of an Accountable Organization

—It's not my job.

—No one told me to do that.

—It's the other department's fault.

Sound familiar? As long as others are busy expressing their defensiveness, frustration and resistance, we can't complete our jobs, customers aren't having their needs met, and the organization is unable to make the changes needed to stay competitive.

Middle Managers in Action

A highly complex and technically-based electronics firm had experienced several years of declining revenue and profits. Senior management made the decision to expand into new market segments that would grow the business and ensure future viability. While this new strategic business direction was on-track for developing new business, the organization wasn't operationally prepared to meet the needs of this new business. Set up in the normal hierarchy with department managers responsible for the performance of their respective departments, the organization continued to fail to meet its revenue goals and performance objectives.

At first, senior management complained that the department managers weren't being accountable enough for the performance of their departments. They would have monthly sessions to review each manager's department and then blame the managers for not meeting the objectives. On the surface, the blame seemed justified. However, upon closer examination, it became evident that the root of the problem lay elsewhere.

While the managers were being held accountable for the performance of their respective departments, no culture existed in the organization for removing non-performers. No individual manager was in a position to begin to deal with non-performance since there was no norm established for doing so. We discovered a basic lack of skill in project management throughout the organization. However, since each middle manager operated within individual silos, they had no idea that it was a systemic problem that could be resolved. Finally, there were conflicting priorities, functional breakdowns and a lack of coordination among departments that never got surfaced or addressed since the managers spent all of their time in their respective departments trying to manage crises and defend poor performance.

We joined middle management into a team with the expanded role of changing the culture and cross-functional processes to improve overall performance. Immediately, the organizational breakdowns surfaced and were resolved. Middle managers developed a strategy for identifying and dealing with non-performers by either coaching them into good performance or assisting them out of the organization through corrective action. Since all managers were doing this together, the change was easier to make. In addition, middle managers established a program to develop all project managers in a consistent manner to support better performance. The conflicts that existed among departments were prioritized by the middle management team and resolved in sub-committees that reported back to the team.

As a result, performance improved significantly within the first six months of change, middle managers were now leading the global operational changes, and all levels of the organization felt a greater sense of cohesiveness and focus on the priorities driving their organizational success.

When we can't count on each other, everyone loses. Regardless of position or function, we must be able to count on each other if we are to succeed.

Accountability involves each individual in the organization regardless of position or function. We all must keep our commitments to perform, our agreements to sustain effective team relationships, and our level of effort given to support others when support is requested or required. In virtually all high-performing teams, teammates help each other out. We see this with music groups learning a difficult piece, baseball teams improving the execution of a double play, theatrical groups memorizing the lines of a production and military units covering for one another. It's the level of accountability that each person demonstrates on a day-to-day basis that builds the morale and the pride of an organization. The confidence that we can count on each other during the rough times is what helps get us through the rough times.

But first, we have to be able to count on ourselves to keep our own commitments. Being accountable depends on **our ability, willingness, courage and commitment to renew our attitudes and behaviors in order to achieve our desired outcomes.** This formula for personal accountability doesn't just apply to the workplace. We also have desired outcomes or goals related to our families, our careers, our personal growth, and our communities. If we become aware of an area in which we are failing to meet our desired outcomes, then we have to ask ourselves, "Do I have the ability?" Usually, our ability reflects what we *thought* was required. For instance, the ability of many people to use a typewriter became obsolete once word processing was introduced. Whether we are talking about our ability to parent well as our children grow older, or our ability on the job with changing technology, we must continue to upgrade our abilities to meet the demands of the future. You probably know people who have reached a plateau with regard to their skills. They think that they have completed learning, growing and evolving.

It's acceptable to find ourselves unable to achieve our desired outcomes so long as we have the willingness to seek the training, coaching, mentoring, or counseling required to gain the ability. In some cases, we can't develop the skills fast enough, and so we may need to call on others in our sphere of influence (such as coworkers and family members) as resources for achieving our desired outcomes. Unfortunately, territorialism in the workplace might prevent us from drawing on someone else's skills to get the job done.

If we lack the willingness to call on others, it is usually due to our ego and pride, which can become a serious roadblock to the achievement of our desired outcomes. It is amazing, yet human, to sabotage our own best interests simply because we have difficulty admitting weaknesses or mistakes.

It takes courage to look in the mirror of personal observation to check out our flaws. It takes commitment to DO something about them by changing our attitudes and behaviors. David McNally speaks of the importance of commitment in his book, *Even Eagles Need a Push*, when he says, "Commitment is the willingness to do whatever it takes to get what you want. A true commitment is a heartfelt promise to yourself from which you will not back down. Many people have dreams and many have good intentions but few are willing to make the commitment necessary for their attainment."[3] Everyone knows people who have been blessed with plenty of talent but who have an

---

[3] David McNally, *Even Eagles Need a Push: Learning to Soar in a Changing World,* Dell Publishing, 1990.

unfortunate attitude of self-righteousness or arrogance that prevents them from achieving their goals.

Success Can Be Our Biggest Obstacle

We all want to be successful. But once we demonstrate some measure of success, we must beware of the trap of thinking that "we have arrived, we have made it, we can rest now." Success is a process, not an event. Whether you are the president of a corporation who assumes that because your organization has sixty percent of the market, it is the secured leader in the industry, or whether you are a senior manager who thinks that your position makes your job secure, you are laboring under the "Success Illusion."

We've all heard stories about entrepreneurs who go belly-up after experiencing great financial success, or straight "A" high school students who later drop out of college because they can't make the grade or because getting "C's" was unacceptable to them. *Attaining success is not nearly as important as sustaining success.* We can sustain success only by responding to the many changes that affect our lives, whether they be changes in technology, changes in customer needs, changes in organizational constraints (such as resources), or changes in competition. On the personal level these include changes in our physical health, changes in our family relationships, changes in our friendships and economic changes. We must continually adapt our skills, attitude and behaviors. Otherwise, we will wake up one day to find that we have lost our position, our money or our relationships and didn't even see it coming.

Employees—From Whiners and Blamers to Customer Activists

Leaders can lead and managers can manage, but without employees, customers aren't served, processes aren't improved, new leaders aren't developed and organizations can't survive. Each employee, regardless of position or title, has a leadership role in contributing to the evolution of an organization. Employees must be activists for change, not only for the sake of the organization, but also for their own sakes.

To be an effective customer activist, we must first be "service" oriented. The rising popularity of customer service over the past decade has been a great first step but, as most of us have discovered, we are all "customers" to one another. Being service oriented is not just about meeting the needs of others; it is also about having the right attitude of helpfulness, assistance, coaching and support. It means replacing the ego-oriented position on which we base our agenda to doing whatever is necessary to get the job done in a manner that supports success for ourselves and for those around us.

Second, we must dedicate ourselves to being the best we can be. Whether we are a manager, a computer programmer, or a clerical administrator, we must look for opportunities to streamline our processes, improve our linkages with those that depend on us, and develop our skills to continue performing at higher levels of excellence. This might mean becoming involved on committees to improve performance or make changes, or offering suggestions to co-workers and upper management regarding how to improve our services, or even cooperating with changes that we don't necessarily like. It also means continually learning, practicing and expanding our skills in order to develop greater confidence in the knowledge that we can handle the unusual and challenging situations that continuously arise. Just like top athletes, musicians and dancers, we will continue to hone our skills.

Third, we must dedicate ourselves to supporting others, especially those whose work will have an impact on, and be affected by us. We must make an effort to understand their needs and constraints. This is critical for effective coordination, cooperation, and sharing of information. We cannot be successful without the support of others, and we must foster that support to be an effective change activist.

Fourth, we must continue to learn new skills outside of our specialty so that we can adapt to those changes that we can't control. We can achieve this through cross-training with others on our teams, taking advantage of workshops and other learning opportunities, and investing in our own personal growth and development in order to increase our awareness and overcome any of our own attitudinal or behavioral blocks. As the amount of change we face continues to increase exponentially, our ability to anticipate those changes becomes even more difficult, and so it is critical for us to continue to "stretch ourselves" in order to maintain and further develop our flexibility and adaptability.

Fifth, we must keep our eye on the future, anticipating changes in our customers, changes in technology, changes in our organization, changes in our personal needs, and any other changes in society that may have an impact on our job, our profession or our career. This is a new skill that every employee should be developing by reading the newspaper and trade journals, talking to upper management and attending meetings with industry specialists.

An organization made up of customer activists like those described here will be able to anticipate future needs, respond to their needs and sustain high levels of performance through the involvement and growth of its work force. However, the benefits extend beyond the organization. Customer activists themselves benefit by acquiring greater self-confidence, greater flexibility, and more nurturing and satisfying relationships with others.

Success is more easily sustained when each level of an organization assumes accountability for its distinct role:

1. Senior managers (catalysts for results and change), who lead and guide the organizational direction and the culture in response to external drivers;

2. Middle managers (change agents), who guide the culture and operations to ensure effective linkages and the removal of unnecessary obstacles; and

3. Employees (customer activists), who are dedicated to improving their relationships with others and their performance as it impacts the customer as well as the organization.

Ultimately, it is each person's responsibility at every position in the organization to be dedicated to their own growth and improvement as well as the support of others improving in the organization. In his book *The Fifth Discipline,* Peter Senge highlights the importance of self-improvement by noting, "At the heart of a learning organization is a shift of mind from seeing ourselves as separate from the world to connected to the world, from seeing problems as caused by someone and something 'out there' to seeing how our own actions create problems we experience."[4] Ultimately, accountability is being accountable for our own actions and improvement to achieve our desired outcomes. With an accountable environment in place, the

---

[4] Peter Senge, *The Fifth Discipline,* Currency Doubleday, 1990.

organization is able to recover quickly—through focus, involvement and dedication at all levels—from any dips in success that may occur.

Figure 5-1: Leadership Roles of an Accountable Organization

LEVELS	ROLES OF LEADERSHIP
SENIOR MANAGERS *ARE* **"CATALYSTS FOR RESULTS AND CHANGE"**	Translate external drivers into a clear Strategic Business Plan. Monitor and guide middle management in achieving operational priorities, improvement projects and operational performance consistent with achieving the outcomes of the Strategic Business Plan.
MIDDLE MANAGERS *ARE* **"CHANGE AGENTS"**	Translate the Strategic Business Plan into a Strategic Operational Plan. Align efforts around the operational priorities, strategize and monitor operational priorities, effectively share resources and develop project plans to achieve the Strategic Operational Plan. Improve the operational infrastructure to remove obstacles and to support employees in performing to satisfy their customers. Assure effective and strategic communications to mobilize the workforce and to develop future leaders according to the changing needs of the organization.
EMPLOYEES *ARE* **"CUSTOMER ACTIVISTS"**	Identify and meet customer expectations. Improve technical processes and individual performance to meet operational priorities established by the Strategic Operational Plan and the changing cultural environment.

⤚ Part 2 ⥲

Five Strategies
for Leading with Accountability

> **Strategy #1:**
> From Empty Vision to Clear Direction
>
> **Strategy #2:**
> Create a Plan that Guarantees Results
>
> **Strategy #3:**
> Communicate to Influence "Non-Believers"
>
> **Strategy #4:**
> Execution: The Key to High Performance
>
> **Strategy #5:**
> Develop Employees
> to Be Accountable High Performers
>
> **Get Started:**
> Your Next Steps to Get Breakthrough Results

⊱ **6** ⊰

Strategy #1:
From Empty Vision to Clear Direction

Myth: Creating the organization's Vision and strategies establishes a clear direction.

Truth: Understanding the External Drivers impacting the organization is necessary for establishing a clear direction.

After experiencing several weight reduction programs in which I lost weight and then regained it, I decided to do something different. I enrolled in a class called Consciousness, Health and Healing from the University of Santa Monica. The instructor asked me for my "picture of success." I repeated the same vision I had developed for my past efforts: "I am thin and fit." The instructor responded, "That is great for your vision and goal, but what is your picture of success?"

Translate Words into Actions

It took me a week to develop, but when complete it read, "I am exercising regularly. I am not using food to escape dealing with challenges or boredom. I don't over-eat by cleaning everything on my plate out of habit, and I am aware of how foods feel in my body in terms of giving me energy or depleting my energy." Without much effort or struggle, within two months of beginning this program I had stopped cleaning every bit of food off of my plate, was aware of how different foods felt in my body and had made the appropriate adjustments. I still over-eat occasionally, but I am on my way to feeling healthier and releasing my weight.

Even the most inspired vision statement is no more than just words on a page. In order for the vision to be achieved it must be brought to life in the form of a clear direction. Otherwise, accountability cannot exist. People must be accountable for something. If there is no outcome to measure against, there can be no accountability.

Max DePree makes this point in his inspiring book on leadership, *Leadership Jazz*: "'Accountable for 'what' and 'to whom?'...are precisely the kinds of questions that so many boards of directors and boards of trustees should be asking themselves. I imagine that quite a few stockholders and faculty members and students would like to hear the answers."[1]

I once interviewed a member of a work unit who had been accused of being hostile towards his co-workers. He didn't deny his hostility; he defended it! "We never agreed to be a team," he asserted. "We never agreed to support one another. If we ever

---

[1] *Leadership Jazz,* by Max DePree. Dell Publishing, 1992.

decide to do so, I'll change my behavior. But until then, I'm going to continue doing whatever it takes to get my job done."

If personal accountability means taking action consistent with one's commitments, then this man was acting with personal accountability. His commitment was simply and solely to get his job done. He had made no commitment to his work group or to anyone else. If commitments aren't made, then no accountability is required. If management doesn't clarify its expectations, then employees can't be held accountable for their performance. Also, if employees don't create their own expectations with each other, then trust, support, and the process for dealing with conflict are never established.

A manager was complaining to me about his team, "People on my team don't support one another. They don't share information with each other and they blame each other constantly." I asked the manager what he does about those problems, and he responded, "Nothing. If they are going to act like children, then I will treat them like children." I asked him how it was working for him. "Terrible," he replied. "They just aren't getting the message." I asked him if they ever established expectations for supporting one another, for not blaming one another and for sharing information. He responded with indignation saying, "Of course not. This is common sense and I shouldn't have to spell it out for them."

After a few months this manager was transferred. The new manager came into the same team and created agreements on teamwork that included how employees would support one another, share information, and resolve conflict. Within a couple of months this low performing and highly complaining team turned into one of the highest performing teams in the company, with the highest levels of trust among employees and management.

When the Words Don't Translate— Prevent Mixed Messages

One of the most common complaints I hear from employees at all levels is that while there's more and more time spent defining the organization's direction through vision statements, strategic plans, Hoshin planning, and so on, they are still confused about the organization's true direction—either because it's too general, or because the actions and decisions within the organization are inconsistent with its stated direction.

Sometimes the confusion arises because management has empowered a *committee* to determine the organization's direction. When this happens the direction is debated according to people's own expertise and their level of comfort with change. Each person brings a distinct perception to the debate, based on his or her internal knowledge of the organization. The person from marketing might think that the organization's new direction should focus on investing more resources in advertising to improve the organization's image. The person in operations who faces morale problems might argue that the new direction should involve investing in capital equipment to address staff complaints. Both have made suggestions that benefit their respective departments, but neither have taken into account what's in the best interest of the organization. Without this global perspective, the suggestions can be debated endlessly.

Integrate Outcomes, Values and External Drivers

Have you ever seen a water faucet with two spouts? One is for hot water, while the other is for cold. The frustration comes from trying to wash your hands with warm water. As long as you put one hand under the hot water and one hand under the cold water, you only get burned. The same is true when we separate business outcomes and mission from the values of the organization. When the business outcomes are separate from the values, then confusion, fragmentation, and competition prevent either one from being achieved.

The ability to define and articulate a clear business outcome and direction depends on three elements, all involving understanding:

1. A clear understanding of the organization's mission in terms of the desired impact on its customers along with the return on investment necessary to be financially viable.

   Most organizations invest time creating a clear Mission Statement, but fall into the trap of thinking that it provides sufficient information to establish an understandable sense of direction. The mission provides only a sense of the *purpose* of the organization. It doesn't reflect the *style* in which the organization will set about to accomplish its purpose.

2. A clear understanding of the organization's values.

   The values of more evolved organizations are clarified with a value statement, which details a consistent set of behaviors intended to guide the culture. Understanding what behaviors are consistent with the organization's values helps clarify its direction. Combining the mission of an organization with its values gives a clearer sense of what it *means* to accomplish the organization's purpose.

3. A clear understanding and response to the "external drivers" affecting the organization.

Important as the mission and the values are, they do not provide employees with a clear sense of direction for how their actions will contribute to the future life of the organization.

When missing, this is the piece that induces people's resistance to change efforts. They have no sense of how they fit into the organization's future plans.

As change speeds up and becomes more global, external factors play an increasing role in defining an organization's direction, a role more critical even than the organization's mission and values. They represent the reason for most of the organization's global changes. *And yet they are rarely communicated*. People are therefore prevented from a full understanding of why many change efforts take place. Instead, they are left with the sense that the organization is fragmented and flailing about in a sea of competition. We will discuss this further in Chapter 7.

These three elements (mission, values, and response to external drivers) are all required in order to develop a clear sense of the organization's direction and business outcomes. The mission relates more to performance, the values relate to the culture that creates the performance, and the external drivers relate to the changes in performance and culture necessary to stay viable. To isolate one element from the others results in a less than complete picture. They must be entirely integrated. But too often, they are addressed in isolation. Robert Kaplan and David Norton explain this necessary integration in their book, *The Balanced Scorecard: Translating Strategy into Action*. They develop a process that focuses on four aspects of performance: the financial perspective, the customer perspective, the internal perspective and the internal business perspective.[2] However, this approach leaves out other external drivers except for the customers, as well as the values that make up the culture of the organization.

---

[2] Robert S. Kaplan and David P. Norton, *The Balanced Scorecard: Translating Strategy into Action,* Harvard Business School Press, 1996.

Success Through Integration

A senior management team of a federal governmental agency in Baltimore needed to accomplish two important business outcomes and felt that their lack of teamwork was a major obstacle to their success. Several consultants had already tried to build the team's working relationship over the previous two years. They had focused on creating more trust, support, cooperation and team decision-making. By the time I was called in, the team was deeply frustrated with the lack of progress.

I knew that the values of teamwork could not be treated separately from business outcomes, so we set up their team system to accomplish their business outcomes while integrating the values of teamwork as they had previously defined them. By the end of six months, they had accomplished their two priority projects. Not only that, their levels of trust, communication, decision-making and cooperation had also improved. In fact, the change was so significant that their employees were also beginning to function with a higher level of teamwork based on the modeling of this senior management team.

The leader of the team was amazed. "For two years we made teamwork our primary focus and didn't accomplish a thing!" he said. "But after making our business outcomes the primary focus and using teamwork as our means, we were able to see the greatest improvements we have ever made."

It is clear that if we are going to create a "Balanced Scorecard," we must identify all the aspects of business that impact the organization. Richard Barrett has done an excellent job of creating a more comprehensive scorecard. He has expanded the original Balanced Scorecard to include six areas. In his book, *Liberating the Corporate Soul,* he describes the creation of the Balanced Needs Scorecard, which includes Corporate Survival, Client/Supplier Relations, Corporate Culture,

Society Community Contribution, Corporate Evolution and Corporate Fitness.[3]

The most common mistake is to treat values independently of mission. Undoubtedly, you can think of at least one organization that has created an entire training and development program that focused the organization on its values, while failing to link those values to the organization's business outcomes (as represented by its mission).

Intention vs. Vision

In order to produce a meaningful, integrated message we need to draw a clear "picture" of the future that people can imagine themselves stepping into. They need to identify with it and be able to see clearly where they will fit in. This is where most vision statements fall short. They usually involve a set of platitudes that express a "commitment" of some sort:

- *To be better than the best.*

- *To exceed the customers' expectations.*

- *To be world class...*

- *To provide the ultimate in customer satisfaction.*

They may sound nice, but when you take a close look at them, they actually mean very little. They don't focus on concrete outcomes. Essentially, they function as rhetoric.

Notice that the word "intention" has the notion of action built right into its definition: "intending; thing intended, purpose."

---

[3] Richard Barrett, *Liberating the Corporate Soul: Building a Visionary Organization,* Butterworth-Heinemann, 1998.

The word "vision," on the other hand, has a passive quality. Like a dream, it is something that "just happens." "Vision" implies that we have very little responsibility to make it happen; "intention" has the full power of the organization's will behind it.

An excellent article by James C. Collins and Jerry I. Porras in the *Harvard Business Review* offers valuable insights into how to build your company's vision: "Vision provides guidance about what to preserve and what to change." It details "a new prescriptive framework" which "adds clarity and rigor to the vague and fuzzy vision concepts at large today."[4] This is what we refer to as the statement of intention.

The scope of a statement of intention exceeds that of a vision statement. A statement of intention presents a full picture. It not only describes what that organization will be achieving in terms of business objectives; it also addresses how its customers will view the organization. It defines the kind of environment in which the organization will operate. And most importantly, it describes how the organization will function to achieve business outcomes, customer outcomes, and to be responsive to change as change intensifies. Gay Hendricks, Ph.D. and Kate Ludeman, Ph.D. refer to the creation of an Intention in their book, *The Corporate Mystic*, "Intention precedes and inspires vision. Intention lives in the zone between potential and action, organizing the diffuse energy of potential and bringing it toward reality...Inspired leadership is the ability to work from the zone of intention, so that your very being brings forth visionary thinking in your colleagues."[5] A statement of intention is a dynamic that is captured in words.

---

[4] *Building Your Company's Vision*, by James C. Collins and Jerry I. Porras, Harvard Business Review, September 1, 1996.

[5] Gay Hendricks, Ph.D. and Kate Ludeman, Ph.D., *The Corporate Mystic*, Bantam Books, 1996.

Scratch the surface of a vision statement and you're likely to find yourself poking through to a hollow core, like one of those chocolate Easter bunnies. A statement of intention has substance. (It's solid chocolate.) It must be stated so vividly as to be almost tangible. It is as thorough as any investigative reporter probing into the who, what, where, when, why and how of company direction.

A statement of intention is characterized by four essential elements:

1. *Responsive.* It identifies the external drivers affecting the organization and how the organization needs to change in order to meet these challenges.

2. *Customer-driven.* It focuses on the organization's distinctiveness by considering how this intention will affect the way in which customers perceive the organization. It identifies the qualities for which the organization will be known.

3. *Action-oriented.* It defines the internal environment that is required in order for the intention to become a reality.

4. *Practical.* It acknowledges how this intention will be of benefit to the financial and long-term viability of the organization and its stockholders.

Unlike the concept of the Balanced Scorecard, an Intention Statement describes the extremes of excellence and leaves open the possibility for paradox. For example, a company can have an intention for high quality and low costs at the same time. In the case of morale, we were able to *increase morale during downsizing,* because we started with a clear intention to achieve that result as a possibility. In the book *Built to Last* by James Collins and Jerry Porras, this is described as "the 'Genius of the AND'—

IMPAQ®'s Own Statement of Intention.

IMPAQ® is part of an increasingly competitive community of consultants ranging from individuals to large organizations. Based on our clients' needs to minimize training costs and become more self-sufficient, it is important for IMPAQ® to further develop its ability to provide Trainer Certification within organizations. Also, the demand in organizations is to move beyond education and training to interventions that demonstrate lasting culture change and a direct impact on business outcomes. Therefore, IMPAQ® will provide a more comprehensive and high end service to its clients in order to assist the organization in making meaningful changes that assure measurable results. In a time where many organizations are experiencing change, IMPAQ® wants to work with organizations that are committed to meaningful changes, which significantly improve business results while supporting the evolution and transformation of its employees.

IMPAQ® is the Innovator and Facilitator of Accountability-Based® cultures throughout organizations and communities worldwide. Our implementation-oriented services link all levels of an organization, produce immediate business outcomes and sustainable improvements, and provide a measurable return on investment. As a result, our clients succeed beyond their established limits of excellence.

We create for ourselves and foster for our clients a supportive environment of commitment, trust, accountability, integrity and continuous improvement, inspired by the heart and spirit of each individual.

We are a successful, profitable and vibrant organization that creates long-lasting partnerships and gives back to its members and to the community in a generous way.

(Notice how each sentence within the statement of intention translates into meaningful outcomes that can be observed, exemplified and measured. IMPAQ®'s intention statement is used for measuring our progress as an organization, as well as for providing a reference for setting priorities, making decisions, and solving conflicts.)

the ability to embrace both extremes of a number of dimensions at the same time. Instead of choosing between **A** *OR* **B**, they figure out a way to have both **A** *AND* **B**."[6]

While a vision statement tends to be static, a statement of intention continues to evolve. The picture that it presents becomes clearer as you move toward it, just as the details of any picture become clearer the closer you are. This is why a statement of intention needs to be updated on a regular basis. At IMPAQ® we update it every year or so. In a fast-paced organization undergoing a lot of change, it may need to be updated every six to nine months. An update, however, isn't a change in direction; it's just a fine-tuning.

Statements of intention are by no means limited in use to the general company; they are useful to formulate at all levels. They can be particularly useful with a leadership team that is trying to break down territorialism and become unified in leading the organization to achieve its business results. There's nothing glib, superficial or purely rhetorical in the following statement of intention developed by a leadership team at one of the leading and most innovative medical centers in the country, St. Charles Medical Center in Bend, Oregon. They used it to become less comfort-oriented, less fragmented and more responsive to the needs of the organization. Six months after creating this statement of intention, their reputation with employees changed and now the medical center's reputation in the national health care community is well established.

---

[6] James C. Collins and Jerry I. Porras, *Built to Last: Successful Habits of Visionary Companies,* Harper & Row, 1997.

Leadership Team Intention Statement
at St. Charles Medical Center

We, the Leadership Team, provide clear expectations to our employees, as well as the growth and development needed to meet them, and the appropriate recognition for their performance. We provide an organized structure for continuous quality improvement, effectiveness of operations and team self-direction. The nurturing environment we create provides the information, resources and culture of team participation needed to allow us to be continually responsive to our customers' needs.

We are a dynamic, action-oriented team willing to take risks for improvement in a responsive environment of mutual trust, respect, accountability and support. Communication and information sharing are open, clear, honest and uninhibited. Clearly defined processes and systems are in place to ensure the highest level of team function and to effectively deal with conflict resolution. Decisions are based on organizational needs and are accurately and consistently represented to all.

We ensure the viability of our organization by being responsive, flexible and accountable to resolve organizational problems and barriers. We ensure that the business plan is achievable and achieved, tying operational systems to business/ financial outcomes and acting on new business opportunities. We exceed community expectations related to care, service and culture.

How would you feel if you were part of the leadership team that developed that statement of intention and measured itself against every sentence? How would you feel if you were an employee whose leadership functioned in a manner consistent with that statement of intention?

Don't Be Fooled...Goals are NOT Outcomes

Nothing causes an organization to become fragmented faster than to treat its goals as desired outcomes. Goals change from year to year—sometimes from month to month—based on the crises that drive new priorities. The desired outcome, on the other hand, always involves an all-encompassing picture of the future. It affects how we accomplish our goals and is the result of what we achieve *after* accomplishing our goals. An organization may identify cutting costs as its primary goal one year. But if it fails to keep sight of its desired outcome (to satisfy its customers), then it may accomplish its goal and go out of business. In this case, the desired outcome involves both strengthening the organization financially and strengthening its reputation with customers. To achieve this outcome, the organization may need to establish a goal to cut costs; the goal is merely one of the steps towards achieving the desired outcome. Goals cannot exist independently of desired outcomes.

Confusing the two leads to unexpected and undesired outcomes. For example, many companies responded to a goal of cutting costs by downsizing its employees and offering an attractive severance package to its senior and more experienced people to encourage them to leave the organization. After people left, they discovered that losing those resources and expertise cost them a loss of customer satisfaction. A year later, some of those organizations had to hire *back* the people that they let go, because of increased demands or the need to improve sagging customer service.

Even in less dramatic situations, when an organization makes cutting costs the goal for one year, improving quality the goal for the next year, job retraining the goal for the next and increasing productivity the goal for the next, we have to wonder:

what is the direction of that organization? As an employee, how do I anticipate the future trends of the organization in order to prepare my skills and mindset for the upcoming challenges the organization will face? How do I fit into an organization that has no sense of identity or purpose? And how do I target my responses to the organization's needs for change when the target is moving randomly from one goal to another?

The Role of Goals

Goals are necessary for translating the outcome and intention of the organization into meaningful and measurable performance objectives. However, the goals must always be subordinate to the outcome and intention of the organization, and should be reviewed in context with the business outcomes, not in isolation. Whatever your goal might be—to increase market share, improve quality, change technology, cut operating expenses, etc.—it is essential to integrate that goal's achievement with your response to other external drivers and to your values as an organization. Only then will people understand the "why" behind the goal. Only then will they be able to identify their own individual objectives for accomplishing the goal in a way that is consistent with the organization's intention. Only then will people be able to see how they fit into the organization after the goal has been achieved.

One year at IMPAQ® we were surprised by a major downturn in our business which occurred just after we had provided people with bonuses for a good year of performance, and invested our cash into new marketing efforts that would boost our business. I went to each of the employees in turn and explained our financial situation. Each offered to have his or her salary cut for a period of one year until the organization could get its feet back on the ground again financially. We stuck together as a team and everyone received bonuses at the end of the year to compensate them for their efforts to save the company. People were able to participate in meeting the challenge because they had a full context for the crisis that we faced.

Bottom Line: Accountability

Most people would agree that the purpose of a vision statement in a traditional organization is to provide a sense of direction, while the purpose of goals is to establish the focus for improvement or achievement. But as we've seen, if that sense of direction isn't clear, or if people become too focused on the micro goals without understanding the context, the vision statement can become a stumbling block.

A statement of intention, however, sets up accountability. *That is its key purpose.* As long as the direction remains vague or unclear, people don't have to be accountable for changing their behavior in order to be consistent with it. Lack of clarity lets them off the hook! Setting a clear intention is not the cure for an organization's lack of accountability or its inability to achieve meaningful business results, but it does provide a foundation without which there would be less effectiveness and greater resistance to change. The statement of intention provides the basis for assessing future decisions, actions, behaviors and attitudes. It acts as a benchmark against which these things can be measured such that they can be modified if they are not in alignment with it. If the intention is unclear, then it's impossible to determine whether something is in alignment with it or not.

∽ **7** ∾

Strategy #2:
Create a Plan that Guarantees Results

Myth: The more we perfect the plan, the more employees accept and are comfortable with change.

Truth: The more we plan for recovery, the more employees accept and are safe to take the risks of change.

Accountability is more than an attitude or philosophy. It's not an "add-on." It cannot be expected to exist in isolation from the way the organization establishes its processes, procedures and policies. This is especially evident when leading changes to achieve breakthrough results.

There's a popular misconception that if we involve people in the planning of change, they will feel accountable for that change. The faultiness of this conception is most readily evident on a micro-level when a group of co-workers turns against a non-performer on their team. They complain to the manager in secret about the non-performer and even complain about the manager who isn't dealing with the non-performer. Yet, when the manager does go through the corrective action process and fires the non-performer, those very same co-workers complain to the manager asking, "How could you do such a terrible thing? We all loved this person!"

You've likely experienced the disruption caused by this misconception on an organizational level as well. For example, a task force of managers and employees recommends restructuring the organization into cross-functional teams. After completing this restructuring, the same people who made the recommendation are the ones who have the most difficulty adapting to the new team structure.

It isn't enough to be involved in the planning of a change to have the accountability for the change and ensure its success. Accountability must be built into each aspect of implementation. It is significant that when an organization implements new performance processes using an accountability-based® approach, the new processes will not only be more successful, they will also transpire more quickly, with more measurable results, and with less resistance.

Six Stages of an Accountability-Based® Implementation

Whether the plan involves a restructure of the organization, the introduction of new technology, new processes and procedures, or even a culture change, certain processes must be completed in order to establish accountability during the change.

In this case "accountability" means the presence of a linkage between people that ensures that results take place. This

is why any implementation must be planned with an appreciation of the natural impact that each stage of change will have on
affected people. It is a mistake to assume that involving more
people in planning, seeking buy-in before implementation, and
empowering people to make necessary changes will eliminate
any resistance or create the accountability required to ensure
success. These approaches do not work because they ignore the
real issues behind people's negative reaction to change.

*Figure 7-1: The table below outlines the stages of change and people's
typical reactions to them.*

STAGES OF IMPLEMENTATION	TYPICAL REACTIONS ⇒	WHICH CAN TURN INTO
1. Planning the Implementation and Communication Strategy	Fear ⇒	Negativity
2. Initial Implementation including Communication	Chaos ⇒	Confusion
3. Clarifying Roles and Relationships	Cooperation ⇒	Frustration
4. Tracking Milestones & Modify	Clarity ⇒	Discouragement
5. Communicating Results	Optimism ⇒	Disbelief
6. Recognizing Success of Implementation and People Involved	Confidence ⇒	Accomplishment

We often fail to complete the process necessary to ensure
measurable results. This is like trying to learn to play songs on a
musical instrument but stopping after only mastering scales.

There is so much more to being a good musician that must be learned and practiced. Unfortunately, we are too busy setting new goals before realizing the old ones. This leaves people frustrated at the ineffectiveness of change and negative about making future changes, which they now perceive as a waste of time and energy.

Some stages are self-explanatory. We will focus on the keys most often missed for effective implementation at each stage, and address specific reactions to these changes that require special attention.

Stage 1: Planning the Implementation and Communication Strategy

Planning is an essential step in any project or change effort. However, with so many failed projects and the degree of resistance from employees, the tendency in recent years has been to "perfect" the plan prior to implementation. Certainly, when an organization is planning the purchase of major capital equipment or construction of a building, it is appropriate to take the time to perfect the plan as much as possible, since recovery is difficult once the commitment is made. However, most projects and change efforts aren't so predictable, and the lengthened planning process can be very detrimental to effective implementation.

Planning Your Way to Failure

Most people not involved in the planning stage would heartily agree that the only thing worse than receiving bad news is receiving NO news. When we don't know where we stand in relation to our situation or our relationships, we feel out of control and enter a state of fear. Anyone who has ever waited for the results of college entrance exams, job applications or medical tests knows how difficult the not-knowing period can be. When we know that changes are going to be made to the structure of an organization, we fear for our jobs. Even if our jobs are secure, we wonder if we will be asked to perform a new function that we don't feel confident about. Furthermore, in a "no news" situation, we tend to imagine the worst.

The longer we are in a "no news" situation, the greater our fear. Our imagination starts working overtime, fueled by stories about the negative experiences of others. A project or change that is still being planned is by definition a "no news" situation. We know that a change is imminent, but don't know how it will impact us directly. By extending the planning period in order to create a more perfect plan which we hope will make people more comfortable, we are actually increasing people's fear about the change. In fact, when the planning stage extends too long, fear can turn into rebellion. This was the case with one organization that planned to restructure. An effort was made to analyze all possible organizational structures in order to create a perfect plan that everyone would accept. Unfortunately, the in-depth analysis took nine months instead of the anticipated three months. In the meantime, employees had grown so rebellious that management decided not to go ahead with the restructuring.

The other downside to "perfect" planning is the impression it gives that if anything goes wrong with the plan, the people implementing the plan must be at fault. This creates even more fear and resistance from employees.

Finally, if our focus is on perfecting the plan, we often fail to even think of developing the *recovery* systems necessary for effective implementation. This means we have become attached to the plan based on how we think it will go, rather than leaving ourselves flexible to adjust as necessary to achieve our desired outcomes. This "detachment" is referred to by Deepak Chopra as the Sixth Spiritual Law of Success in his book, *The Seven Spiritual Laws of Success*, "The Law of Detachment says that in order to acquire anything in the physical universe, you have to relinquish your attachment to it. This doesn't mean you give up your intention, and don't give up your desire. You give up your attachment to the result (as you planned it)."[1] Becoming "detached" to our plan enables us to stay open when the unexpected takes place and adjustments are necessary.

Accountability-Based® Planning—A Shortcut to Success

Figure 7-2 illustrates the benefits of accountability-based® planning. Notice that the time involved is the same for both traditional and accountability-based® planning. But accountability based planning requires a shorter planning stage and involves the development of recovery systems. Consequently, fear is reduced and implementation takes place sooner. This means that results become evident sooner as well. The "extra" time can then be devoted to modifying the implementation based on experience rather than theory.

---

[1] Deepak Chopra, *The Seven Spiritual Laws of Success: A Practical Guide to the Fulfillment of Your Dreams,* Amber-Allen Publishing and New World Library, 1993.

Figure 7-2: Traditional vs. Accountability-Based® Planning

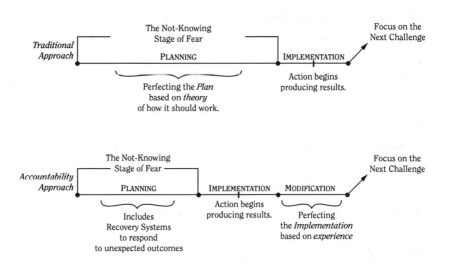

By focusing more on the development of recovery systems than on the perfection of the *plan*, we have been able to reduce the time required to develop plans and begin change by up to 50% *and* achieve greater results after implementation. The truth is, it is impossible to perfect any plan without first taking action.

So, while we can't anticipate all the problems that might surface, we can establish contingency plans and ways to mobilize resources when problems do surface. Focusing on recovery eliminates the worry that people will be punished for mistakes. This frees them up to concentrate instead on developing responsive and timely solutions. Nowhere was this better demonstrated than in the space expedition to Mars in the spring of 1997. The computers were down and needed repair while the expedition was in progress. Fortunately, recovery had been a critical part of the planning process. Heroes emerged among those individuals who were ready to respond to such a challenging and unpredictable situation.

The Steps to Creating a Plan that Achieves Results

1. ***Clear Outcome.*** Prior to initiating a plan, it is important to have a clear picture of success. What would be accomplished once the implementation is complete?

2. ***Success Factors and Measurable Indicators.*** It is not only important to identify the measurable results that are desired after implementation of the plan, but it is also important to understand what success will look like from a functional perspective. This means developing clear statements describing what it looks like to be accomplishing and implementing the plan successfully in addition to the measurable indicators. For example, one success factor could include how various people cooperate and complete their assignments on time to support the implementation effort.

3. ***Milestones for Success and Timing.*** Once we understand the outcomes and the success factors, it is important to create a set of completion targets that will indicate whether or not the implementation is on track. Milestones present a roadmap for accomplishing the plan and provide the means for tracking the results as progress is made. I wouldn't make a cross-country trip by car from Los Angeles to New York without first knowing which cities I would be stopping at along the way, and the timing of those stops.

4. ***Challenges, Obstacles and Constraints.*** Identifying the challenges that could arise in the future and prevent success is rarely done, but is one of the most important aspects of a successful plan. Too often, we wait until implementation begins to identify obstacles, and then only to find that it is too late to deal with them. Once these

challenges are identified, we can determine the ones that are within are influence and those which aren't. If there are too many obstacles, we may decide to trim down our expectations and scope of our plan in order to prevent failure.

5. ***Actions to Achieve the Milestones.*** Once the milestones and obstacles are clear, we can identify the actions that will accomplish the plan. These actions must not only assist in achieving the first milestone, but must also be proactive to address future milestones if appropriate. Also, these actions must address the obstacles discussed earlier.

6. ***Recovery Process.*** Developing a recovery process is one of the most important steps but one that most often gets forgotten. What kinds of problems may occur that we can't predict? What if several unpredictable obstacles happen at the same time? A recovery plan identifies various types of breakdowns including performance breakdowns, relationship breakdowns and changes occurring from outside of the project. Then, a recovery plan is established which identifies what resources are needed and how they will be mobilized to get back on track to successfully complete the plan.

7. ***Follow-up Accountability.*** With the action plan complete, it is important to develop a follow-up plan according to the milestones. An action plan informs all involved team members of the progress of the implementation according to the agreed upon milestones. If a milestone is complete on time, then the team can brainstorm solutions in alignment with the recovery plan already in place.

8. ***Evaluation and Recognition.*** Once the implementation is complete, it is critical to measure the results in comparison with the desired outcomes. Once we have this feedback, we can acknowledge success and the people involved, and examine the areas that could have been smoother such that performance next time could be im-

proved. Ultimately, it is this step of the plan that will turn non-believers into believers.

Once the plan is complete, the next critical part, which is often short-changed, is the development of a communication strategy to inform others of the plan. I have seen some project initiatives take three to six months to communicate, while at the opposite extreme other initiatives are communicated by email. Both methods are ineffective. Taking too long to communicate the plan creates more confusion than clarity, especially since many project solutions or changes aren't understood until actual actions are taken that allow people to experience the results. Also, taking an overly long amount of time to communicate the plan only further extends the planning period, which increases the state of fear. On the other hand, communicating an important change via email or some other form that does not allow for back and forth dialogue leaves people's questions unanswered, creating confusion, frustration and resistance.

Communication is not an event. It is an on-going process that needs to be delivered throughout all the stages of implementation. It should be coordinated in such a way as to produce a unified message. A good communication strategy is based not on how well we share information, but on how well we manage the inevitable reaction to that information. We will discuss the communication strategy in greater detail in Chapter 8.

Finally, whenever we make plans that we fail to implement, we create an environment of negativity that undermines confidence in management's ability to lead. George Bush's now memorable phrase "Read my lips" promised a plan of no new taxes during his administration. His failure to implement that plan led to a catastrophic decline in his support.

Stage 2: Accountability-Based® Implementation

Implementation requires much teamwork, support, and cooperation. Yet, managers frequently "empower" others to implement their "perfect" plan, only to find themselves with stalled efforts and failed results.

Hiding Behind Empowerment

"We have studied the problem at great length, developed an in-depth plan, and now *YOU* are empowered to implement the plan we have given you."

Does that sound familiar? Not only do we feel a little lost by the change that catapults us out of our comfortable way of performing the job, but we also feel abandoned by management which has now empowered *US* to solve all the problems when, in fact we still need direction and guidance from them.

After planning comes action, and the sooner action is taken the better. However, we must bear in mind that no matter how well we plan, the initial stage of implementation will be chaotic. Chaos is inevitable because at this stage people are either implementing new processes, working with new people, or using new technology. Whenever we do something new we must expect a learning curve until we are proficient. We'll be slower than we were before the change was implemented. We'll be awkward and will make mistakes as we adjust to the changes. Yet, during this stage of awkward, slow learning, we will still have customers to satisfy and they will still be expecting the same level of responsiveness and quality as before. So we will feel pressured as well, which will add to the turmoil.

Such chaos is consistent with the laws of nature. Imagine you are sitting in front of a still pool of water. Drop a pebble into the water and observe the chaos. Then watch the chaos settle down into ripples radiating out from the place where the pebble entered the water. Now toss a second pebble into the water so that it disrupts the pattern of ripples. Chaos ensues once again. But before long, even the two sets of ripples settle down into a new and predictable pattern.

Lead Through Chaos and Crisis

Recovery plans help us to shift from being reactive to being proactive when an organizational change is introduced. An unexpected problem occurring in the initial stages of implementation can easily turn the chaos into complete crisis. However, if recovery systems were created during the planning stages, people will be prepared for crisis and cope with it much more effectively. The good news about chaos and crisis is that at least they shift our focus from paralyzing fear regarding the full range of "what if" scenarios into action regarding the "what is" scenario. A focus on recovery helps turn the confusion and surprise of chaos into predictable actions, and this has a calming effect on everyone involved.

Many projects or change efforts come to a halt after the implementation stage. Managers either begin planning the next project or react to the crisis caused by the existing one. This causes problems about three months into the implementation when the crises are diminishing and people have settled into new routines. People now find themselves confused about the real differences created by new processes of the change effort.

Though processes, technology, or teammates may have changed, people find themselves conducting their same job in a similar way as to how they performed it prior to the change. This is when the goals of the project or change effort are most at risk and likely to be compromised; people have a tendency to return to their old ways of doing things.

Some examples are as follows: Managers who have been restructured into a team are still making decisions autonomously; the newly formed cross-functional team of employees is still not sharing critical information to achieve better results on the job; employees forget what it was, exactly, that the project or change effort was supposed to accomplish. They're not sure about their new roles and relationships, and realize they can do their job in a way that is very similar to the old, comfortable way. Without making a conscious decision to do so, they slip back into their old habits of behavior and attitude. The net result, when the project or change effort stops after implementation, is that three to six months later people will see the effort as having been superficial or a waste of time.

Stage 3: Clarify Roles and Relationships

Although general roles and relationships are addressed at the beginning of stage two, they need to later be clarified and refined to reach even a greater level of detail now that people have had a chance to experience the realities of the new situation.

Success Depends on Effective Linkage

I worked with one manager who complained about the difficulties of project implementation in her organization. I mentioned that one of the keys to successful implementation is to clarify roles and relationships. She assured me that this stage had been already completed. But I knew from her descriptions of the confusion and the breakdowns of teamwork that we were not talking about the same thing when it came to clarifying roles and relationships.

Her description of this step went on as follows: "Everyone on the team was brought into a conference room. They took turns reading aloud their job roles, job descriptions and job duties. Everyone asked questions about everyone else's responsibilities to gain a full understanding of the project." While this might have been a good starting point, it didn't address or clarify the linking relationship between each role.

It is critical to determine and clarify how people are going to function differently with each other in their new roles. This involves dissecting the linkage between people. While I may know what your responsibilities are in your new role, I don't know what information you need from me, or what decisions must be involved. Stage three serves to solidify implementation in these ways, and thus optimize results. At this point, expectations are clarified, boundaries are discussed, and needs are articulated and discussed.

This is the time for team members to create agreements regarding the specifics of their own team dynamics — namely how they will share information, resolve conflicts, make decisions, and hold each other accountable when they fall back into pre-change patterns of behavior. They then establish a means of monitoring their results as a team by establishing specific milestones that demonstrate progress made. Any team that *does not make the time* to manage this *post-implementation* clarifying process will find itself stuck in old behavior patterns and unresolved conflicts.

Stage three is when true accountability for making the change takes place. Confusion is now replaced with a sense of cooperation and collaboration. Clarifying expectations, and understanding how we will function together, result in a sense of teamwork not often experienced in organizations. Now that the linkages we depend on to achieve high performance are in place, we no longer feel that our lack of performance is the result of another team member's lack of cooperation.

But we're not finished with the change process yet. Stopping at this stage will eventually result in frustration. Until we put the process outlined here into practice, we can't know for sure if the agreements we've made are the ones we need to help us to function effectively as a high performance team. Most likely, we will need to modify, or at least fine-tune, our agreements and our relationships based on the practicalities of the workplace. For example, one team member may become unable to attend meetings because of her travel schedule, while another may not be available to participate in all decisions because she will be out in the field. If these adjustments aren't made, then everyone grows frustrated in the wake of another failed agreement, and they experience the misunderstandings, hurt feelings and resentments that arise when the team is breaking down.

Stage 4: Track Milestones and Make Modifications

While accountability is established in Stage 3, accountability becomes operational in stage 4. True accountability is tested when mistakes are made or when systems or agreements break down. Do people quit? Do they attack one another? Do they ignore problems? Or do they immediately surface issues and problems along with solutions? Do they hold each other accountable in a supportive way to get back on track? Without milestones to measure progress, many projects or change efforts lack the accountability necessary for full success.

Have the Guts to Face Breakdowns

Based on the agreements developed in Stage 3, regular meetings are held to monitor milestones and modify processes, functions and relationships. Now is the time to see what is and is not working based on tangible expectations and measurable results. We need regular opportunities to surface, discuss and solve problems. During these meetings, decisions are made with clear actions and commitments to taking those actions in order to improve performance. Agreements regarding the functioning of the team are reviewed and modified. Any lack of accountability is surfaced and discussed in order to achieve greater success and an even higher level of support during the next period.

An odd phenomenon takes place during Stage 4 which is generally about five to seven months after the change has been implemented. Every team and organization with which we have worked has experienced a state of discouragement during Stage 4. In its manifestation it can be as obvious as depression or as subtle as apathy. Strangely, it doesn't seem to make any difference how successful the project has been in terms of well-defined measurable results; people still tend to experience discouragement at this stage. So far, there has been no way to prevent this reaction. The only antidote seems to be to move on to the next stage, Stage 5, where it is addressed.

Stage 5: Communicate Results

One reason that we become discouraged during our change efforts is because we focus so keenly on what needs modification and improvement. Month after month we examine what *isn't* working and consider how to make modifications to improve results. It's understandable how we can become discouraged.

Implementation always gives rise to problems that were not anticipated or included in the plan.

The Discouragement Trap

I worked with a team that was very frustrated because their conflicts were never acknowledged, and thus could never be resolved. The members were tired of the hidden agenda that was part of every communication. No one felt safe. So we created a process for surfacing and dealing with conflict in a more supportive manner.

When I returned three months later, they complained that things were even worse than before. Luckily, I'd had them complete a survey before we started and then once again at this follow-up session. I showed them the results of the surveys, which indicated that they had, in fact, significantly improved their levels of trust, communication, participation, and conflict resolution. They realized that they had forgotten what it was like before. As one member shared, "Now that we are surfacing and dealing with our conflicts it just *appears* that we have more conflict than ever." The other members agreed. After a few minutes of discussion, the group grew noticeably optimistic about their progress as a team. Encouraged by their measurable improvement, they wanted to take on many more performance objectives now that they had demonstrated the ability to work through their differences.

With change efforts that involve more tangible performance criteria, the illusion of failure is even more prevalent. Figure 7-3 indicates how, as time progresses, the positive energy that comes from solving the most immediate change-related problems turns into discouragement and apathy. The honeymoon is over. A similar phenomenon occurs after we marry, after we purchase a new home or after we get a new job. And for some reason, it usually takes place around 6 to 12 months after a major change.

Figure 7-3: How our attitudes shift 6-12 months after a major change.

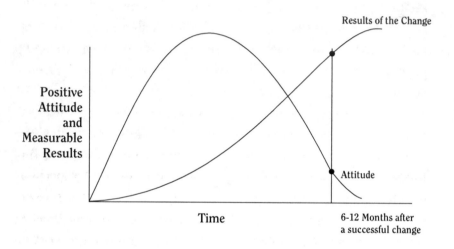

This corresponds to another trend that we have identified. The measurable and tangible results of a change effort are actually at their highest levels about 6 months to 12 months after the project or change is implemented. This is because it takes a certain amount of time for results to become evident. During initial implementation, when people are experiencing chaos and crisis, the results are minimal. They increase exponentially as they build upon one another. However, because our focus in Stages 3 and 4 is on those areas requiring the most improvement and having the highest rate of failure to meet expectations, we become discouraged.

The Importance of Keeping Score

In November 1995 I helped to implement a change in Lagoven/ PDVSA, a large Venezuelan oil company. They were having problems related to performance and productivity. We set up milestones, expectations and agreements for making improvements. In addition, we identified over a hundred unresolved conflicts among departments. I was scheduled to return in March to measure their progress. In February, they called to say that they hadn't had enough time to implement the changes they had committed to, and so we rescheduled our follow-up for May. In May, they called to reschedule the follow-up for August, giving me the same excuse. It was clear to me that they were discouraged and didn't want to face their perceived failure. I was reminded of a comment by one of my coaches, Tracy Quinton: "You may think you are losing when you are actually winning, if you don't keep score."

I knew that I had to take a strong stand and come in May as scheduled. When I arrived, they completely changed my schedule in order to prevent me from doing my follow-up assessment. After readjusting my schedule and finally conducting my assessment, we discovered that 60% of the performance expectations that had been identified showed significant improvement. In addition, 55% of all unresolved conflicts were completely resolved as agreed by all parties both separately and privately. This shocked upper management as well as the rest of the organization. But the most amazing results were in the tangible changes that had taken place since the implementation of change. Each manager could demonstrate measurable improvements in organizational performance and productivity.

Given their level of discouragement, how long do you think it would have taken for them to abort this change and start another change effort, which would lead to even greater frustration and discouragement? Now we can see another reason why "flavor-of-the-month" changes take place in organizations—often people don't realize just how much improvement has actually occurred.

Communicating the results is the most critical step for sustaining measurable and meaningful improvements and keeping employees motivated and encouraged during implementation. If we stop short of this step, people will begin to discount the measurable results and to question their validity. This is when disbelief sets in within the minds of those involved in the project or change effort.

Stage 6: Recognize Success and the People Involved

After communicating the organizational results of the project or change, it is important to draw the link between those results and the measurable business outcomes which formed the basis of the project. This step adds meaning to the effort and reminds people of how the intention of the organization relates to external drivers, to internal values and to the mission of the organization. Nothing is more motivating than being part of an organization that can demonstrate that it has accomplished its clearly stated purpose through a well-coordinated and unified effort. Everyone shares a great sense of accomplishment when the organization succeeds through determined actions as opposed to just pure luck of the marketplace.

The Essential Element of High Morale: Making a Difference

It is important to recognize the *results* prior to recognizing the *people* who achieved those results. Otherwise, the recognition is empty. For example, some groups have been recognized for their effort only to discover that they didn't get results and now don't have a job.

Ultimately, *people want to know that they have made a difference*. Simply being told we did a good job doesn't tell us that our efforts made a difference. Once we understand the impact our efforts had on creating meaningful changes, we really appreciate recognition for those efforts and for the contribution we made to the organization's success. As part of this recognition, it is critical to acknowledge the breakdowns that occurred and the recovery processes which people used, since this best illustrates their level of commitment and dedication to excellence. Also, this is a time to reinforce the linkages that were created between people, levels, departments and functions in order to ensure success.

In short, it is essential to link these changes made in the culture to the measurable results which indicated achievement of business outcomes. This comprehensive approach to recognition builds trust, commitment and motivation, and it delivers a clear message to those employees who are still not aligned with the transformation.

Recognition not only brings a sense of closure, it also inspires in people a sense of accomplishment that will carry them into the next project or change effort. By posing the organization's intention statement as the basis for recognition, we provide people with an update as to the next set of habits that need to be transformed. This second set of changes, however, will flow naturally from the previous project rather than standing alone as yet another separate and fragmented "flavor-of-the-month." Most importantly, based on their now previous success of overcoming obstacles, people at all levels emerge with a feeling of confidence, an understanding that perfection wasn't necessary, and a sense of self-empowerment to tackle the next change effort with less fear and resistance.

∞ **8** ∞

Strategy #3:
Communicate
to Influence "Non-Believers"

Myth: Change should not be implemented without buy-in.

Truth: True buy-in comes after implementation, when people have experienced the results of the change.

When my daughter was six years old she became enamored with the idea of ice-skating. She had never skated before but was inspired by the ice skaters she saw on television during the Olympics. She begged us unrelentingly to take her skating and after a couple of weeks we did. When we arrived, she was excited but a little overwhelmed by the different environment of the cold rink. Her first setback was putting on her skates, but that was nothing compared to the struggle she experienced when she tried to stand up. That's when she informed us that she didn't want to skate anymore. She demanded that we go home. Knowing that she had a history of not liking new activities at first but loving them after getting used to them, we told her that we were planning to stay until she tried to skate. At the same time, I reassured her that I would be on the ice with her to hold her up and make sure she wouldn't fall. She was resistant and shed some tears, but this was typical for her when trying something new. We went around the rink once, and she cried most of the time, but she didn't fall. I complimented her on her courage and persistence and told her I was proud of her. Based on our agreement, we accommodated her request and went home.

The following weekend I decided to take her ice-skating again, since I didn't want her to leave this sport with a bad feeling or with a fear that would prevent her from trying it again. This time she cried again but was receptive to my giving her a skating lesson. Although she continued to cry during the lesson, she managed to skate across the rink all on her own without falling down. Again, I complimented her on her progress and success, and her courage to keep trying even though she was crying.

By the end of the month, her crying had been replaced by laughing, joy, and well-deserved pride—she now counted up to 94 times that she had skated around the rink on her own without stopping or holding on. While skating has not become her favorite activity, she overcame her fear to the point where she enjoys it enough to ask us to take her four or five times a year.

My daughter's desire was to skate. But even with that desire, she still had to move through her own wall of fear. Once the fear took over, she didn't want to skate anymore. Like most of us, once fear takes over, she stopped moving toward her desired goal. The only way for her to overcome her fear was to get on the ice and skate. No amount of watching other skaters on television or reading her stories about skating was going to reassure her. By taking action one step at a time, with safety and guidance, she was able to be successful. This was her accountability in action.

The Moment of Truth

Almost anyone who has worked in upper level management in the past decade has, at some point, been part of a team to plan the implementation of a major change initiative that has impacted every person in the organization. We've all "been there," and it probably looked something like this: We spent several months analyzing the situation, researching different approaches for improving the situation and solving the issues that created the need for the change in the first place. We involved people from all levels of the organization and even included external experts to make sure we hadn't missed anything that could potentially cause failure. We understood all the factors that went into the philosophy behind the change. We solved problems and dealt with conflicts regarding different approaches for implementation. We were confident that the plan was well thought out, with supporting data and clear steps for implementation. Then we faced the moment of truth, when the plan turned into action.

This is where the rubber meets the road. We know that our proposed recommendations will impact the lives of many people, including ourselves. We have no idea how people will react or respond to our recommendation. What we do know is that communication of the implementation plan may be the single most important factor in determining its success or failure. No matter how much time is spent planning, if the implementation plan is poorly communicated or is misunderstood, it will result in complete failure and we will have to abort the effort and start all over. No wonder we lose sleep worrying about how to communicate in a way that generates support and participation.

We've all heard horror stories about the ineffective communication of major change initiatives. I will never forget Dave, a participant in one of my workshops on change management about ten years ago, who described the most recent organizational improvements in which he was involved. Dave happened to be one of the union members of a U.S. auto manufacturer. He was selected to serve on a task force to study the implementation of a Quality of Work Life Program that would benefit all employees as well as the company. The members of the task force analyzed the best programs and the best ways to implement the program throughout the organization. They made a special effort to elicit the support and buy-in of the union as well as the various levels of management. As soon as senior management approved the task force's recommendation, the change was announced to all employees. Dave was reduced to tears as he described how it was announced by means of a *memo* sent by management to all employees. The memo offered no explanation and no opportunities for discussion. As a result, it met with complete resistance from employees. He lamented the fact that this had been a wonderful program that had to be scrapped before it ever had a chance to be implemented, all because of poor communication. Seven months of effort completely thrown away. Unfortunately, this scenario is all too familiar.

While taking too *little* time to prepare an effective communication can result in failure, taking too *much* time to communicate can be equally disastrous. This was the case when a major restructuring was planned at a large petroleum company. Because of the widespread impact that would result from the change, the plan was to communicate it to all employees by means of small discussion groups led by members who were directly involved with the restructuring. In order to reach all ten thousand employees in the organization, the communication took place over a three-month period and had the goal of eliciting buy-in for the proposed restructure. However, during this period many questions arose regarding the proposal and its implementation, and these questions remained unanswered, producing a growing skepticism among employees.

As a result, the task force reconvened to decide how to answer the questions. Once again the task force met with each of the employees in discussion groups. By this time the communication of change was approaching the six-month mark. Now the task force faced even greater cynicism and negativity because employees had discussed the restructuring among themselves for a period of several months, stirring up greater negativity and even more unanswered questions. By the time the task force members completed their discussions, they were forced to abort the restructuring effort that had taken a year to plan and six months to communicate.

These days most of us tend to take more time to communicate than is needed, but we are so nervous about facing the negativity and resistance involved with the announcement that we have made eliciting "buy-in" the underlying purpose of our communication. We want to make sure that everyone likes the change and is comfortable with it before we implement it.

Going for Buy-In: The Trap Preventing Effective Implementation

For many years I, too, was an advocate of eliciting buy-in from everyone involved before implementing a change. And in fact buy-in *is* critical when improvements are made at the employee level regarding the procedures and technical equipment which make up the "tools" employees use to perform their jobs. It does make sense to get buy-in from all employees when decisions are made to improve their equipment or work processes. However, for improvements involving more global issues, such as restructuring, purchasing new computer equipment, or changing of processes which impact the organization's culture, eliciting buy-in prior to making the change is less effective and can actually be very detrimental to its success.

Indeed, the theory behind eliciting buy-in before moving forward on a project is logical enough. When people agree with a change they have an easier time supporting and making the change. If, in the process of getting buy-in, employees make some modifications to the plan, then the implementation will probably just be improved upon, the overall process will encounter less resistance and reduced frustration, and the overall implementation will take less time. This makes sense, right?

Wrong! When a *mindset* change is necessary for implementing a new organizational structure, a new technology, or new global processes and procedures, then making buy-in the purpose of communication can be a "death trap." What makes a mindset change different from other changes is that it requires us to view the project from a new perspective. When we are stuck in our old familiar perspective, we don't see the value of the new mindset. We have to experience it in order to grasp its value. Even the best sales pitch won't make a difference. What's worse, focusing on achieving buy-in as the primary purpose of your communication of a new mindset will actually delay the experience of the new mindset. It is only through experiencing the solutions that we will achieve breakthrough results and prevent the natural resistance associated with adopting the new mindset. This is one of the great paradoxes of leadership. The intention to achieve greater support by trying to elicit buy-in prior to implementation often creates even more resistance.

The Impact of Fear on People's Resistance to Change

As the economist John Kenneth Galbraith once said, "Faced with the choice between changing one's mind and proving that there is no need to do so, almost everybody gets busy on the proof."

Most of us are inclined to resist change. Perhaps there's a natural law at work that parallels the law of inertia in physics. In *WordPower,* his dictionary of vital words, preeminent lateral thinker Edward de Bono defines inertia as "the willingness of things to stay exactly as they are unless moved by sufficient force. We know that this is so in physics and yet we are surprised when it turns out to be the case with organizations."[1]

Communication is the transition from Planning (Stage 1) to Implementation (Stage 2), both discussed in detail in Chapter 7. People react to the planning stage with fear. This is the natural response to being in a situation of "not knowing," which leaves us feeling insecure and out-of-control about our future. It gives rise to worrying, and this encourages our own "what if" scenarios about the future. It is a normal survival behavior to anticipate danger. We respond by thinking about all the possible problems before it happens.

Similar dynamics were at work when one of my well-intentioned friends warned me, many years ago, about getting into the consulting business. "Most likely you won't be successful," he predicted, "since so many people go out of business in their first five years. However, if you *are* successful, then you'll

---

[1] Edward de Bono, *Wordpower,* Penguin, 1990.

probably fail because you'll need to depend on other employees who won't be able to perform to your satisfaction or to the satisfaction of your clients." He was, of course, only "looking out for my best interests" and attempting to protect me from what he saw as certain failure. People who are faced with change also face their fear of the unknown.

It is normal human behavior to avoid fear by running away, procrastinating, or sabotaging the person who is instituting the project or change effort. This is evident in relationships where one person "can't" commit, when we plan to start our diet "tomorrow," or when we avoid starting a project that seems overwhelming. Procrastination and sabotage are the tactics of choice when it comes to avoiding change. When we know that management is holding out for our buy-in before initiating the change, what is the obvious strategy for slowing down or aborting the change? Refuse to buy-in!

Sometimes I'm convinced that everyone has read the same manual on how to avoid implementation, whose instructions are simple and as follows: *By constantly asking questions about the project, raising doubts about the project, and requesting that managers prove that it will work, you can postpone the implementation indefinitely.* How many times have you seen a project planned and then postponed so that more research can be done, or so that a survey can be conducted? How many times have you seen new task forces created since old ones failed to convince people of the importance of a project?

Ironically, such delay tactics prove to be far more painful than the process of implementing the project. The anticipation of implementation is almost always worse than the implementation itself because until it begins to take place, people find themselves fighting phantoms.

Involvement vs. Buy-In

Involvement is not the same as buy-in. Involvement focuses on *how* the change will be made. Buy-in focuses on *whether* the change should be made. After spending several months assessing the need for a change and planning its implementation, the last thing we need to do is to extend the discussion of whether or not we should make the change. Ultimately, there is no right or wrong answer to that question since none of us can predict the future. And, when people are nervous about the future, they will most likely choose comfort over risk and decide, in the end, to keep things the same.

This doesn't mean that we don't need input from affected parties—input is critical for the decision-makers to have a full perspective. But the new direction for the organization is a larger issue that is based on a multitude of external drivers that not everyone in the organization will fully understand because it isn't the nature of their job to see the big picture. Everyone will perceive the proposed outcomes in the context of his or her own particular perspective. There are natural limitations to each person's perspective regardless of their position or level in their organization. Each person's perspective is shaped by the need to attend to the details of their own particular job. Most won't be able to see the forest for the trees; nevertheless, their ability to see every knot on every branch of every tree is essential to the smooth, effective operation of the organization. Similarly, while upper management is in a position to be able to see the full, panoramic view, their ability to see the trees in detail may well be limited. That's precisely why they need input from employees in order to make responsible decisions.

Moreover, most changes involving the future direction of the organization come from external rather than internal influences. Competition is changing, customers are changing, government regulations are changing, and technology is changing. These are all external drivers that influence the need for the organization to change. The people working in the organization are focused internally. Their perspective is most useful when it comes to *translating* the new direction into a meaningful operation plan in their own area. So naturally we want them involved in implementing the change; but not in deciding the direction of the organization, since that's not the perspective that they're coming from.

A Place for Buy-In

This is not to say that buy-in isn't desirable. The question is: When is the appropriate time for expecting buy-in? When we announce a recommendation at the beginning of implementation, we are presenting our "theory" of the best way to make things better. We don't yet know if our theory will work. How quick are you to accept a theory before you have had a chance to see it in practice? Most of us want first to see proof that the theory works before we buy-in to it.

I used to think that the second stage, implementation, was the ideal place for buy-in. Since actions speak louder than words, I assumed that people would buy-in to the recommended solutions when they saw that management was serious about taking actions to implement those proposed solutions. However, when we examine what the common reactions are to each stage of change, we find that the beginning of implementation is not the best time since people are in a state of chaos, and sometimes crisis. It doesn't make sense to expect buy-in when people are experiencing the highest degree of breakdown on their jobs.

Genuine buy-in follows experience. How many people believed we were actually going to get a person to walk on the moon before we actually saw it happen on television? Until then, it was a vision that some people believed possible while others did not. The optimal communication time for eliciting buy-in is at Stage 5, **Communicating Results of Implementation.** Only when people can reflect on their own actual experience with the change can they truly buy-in to it.

Communicating the results of the implementation, however, involves more than relaying the successes of the solution. This would be akin to "selling" its success, which, because it is perceived as manipulation, creates more doubt than confidence. People know that no solution is perfect, so it is important to communicate the difficulties and failings of the solution as well as the successes. It is also important to communicate the plans for dealing with those difficulties and failings. Communicating the successes, failings and plans to improve the failings shows honesty and credibility on the part of management; qualities that are too often lacking in today's organizations.

Most importantly, management also demonstrates commitment by acknowledging that they are still committed to the solution *in spite of* its imperfections, and intends to address those drawbacks in order to stay on course. Commitment is a vital ingredient. It is unreasonable to expect employees to buy-in to the success of the solution or to pretend it's perfect for the organization. Everyone knows that this solution won't be perfect and that it will have to be modified to be successful. And they know that in years to come it will eventually become outdated and be replaced by the next change. Ultimately, employees are buying into management's commitment to the change, and into their commitment to deal with the inevitable problems that will arise. Why should we expect people to invest the effort required to make the solution successful if management is going to throw away its commitment at the first sign of imperfection, only to replace it with the next "flavor-of-the-month" change?

There's another critical reason why Stage 5 is the best time for communication of results: it is at this time that the affected employees will be feeling the most discouraged. This is when employees need to be reassured that, despite problems and failings, the change is, in fact, producing the desired results. Discouragement can be transformed into buy-in and optimism by demonstrating unified commitment and making a clear statement to those people not supporting the solution to either get on board or to find a new train to ride. Buy-in *is* a critical step in any change process and it is precisely at Stage 5 when people need their spirits lifted. It acknowledges their accomplishments and renews their commitment to solving the problems that have surfaced.

Communicate to Inspire Action

Let me introduce you to three types of people who can be readily identified in any corporate change effort. First, there are "active supporters" who like change or believe in management enough to trust the changes that arise to better the organization. They will actively support new solutions no matter what they are. Second, there are "Negativists" who are comfortable with the status quo and tend to be chronic devil's advocates or complainers, viewing the glass as half empty even when it's three quarters full. They can be counted on to actively negate and resist the new solution no matter how well it is communicated. Finally, we meet the "silent skeptics," who have a wait-and-see attitude about the solution. They form the majority, and don't express any opinion.

Both the active supporters and the negativists openly express their views. They like to be visible, whereas the silent skeptics prefer to stay invisible as long as possible. They are the ones who will duck in a classroom or a team meeting in which the facilitator asks for volunteers to participate.

Guess what group usually gets the most attention when we are communicating new solutions? The negativists. They, of course, also ask the most challenging questions. We kid ourselves into thinking that if we address all of their concerns and questions, we will be able to convince everyone that the planned solution is going to be successful. However, the negativists aren't trying to win that argument. They don't need to. They can effectively sabotage the success of the solution simply by raising doubts in the minds of others. Since no one can predict the future, the negativists create as much doubt as possible in order to arouse fear among the silent skeptics who are just waiting for an excuse to become negative so that they can remain comfortable as well. The longer we address the negativist's unanswerable questions and concerns, the longer people pick up the negativity, doubt and fear that goes along with this kind of exchange. Therefore, the negativists are the *last* group in which we want to focus our efforts at eliciting support and cooperation for the change. This doesn't mean that we ignore this group. It simply means that we don't give them any more attention in our communication than we give anyone else.

It may appear that the best strategy of communication would be to address the active supporters. Surely, by addressing the supporters of the solution, a positive momentum will be created that will encourage others to participate in the change. However, while negativists have great influence on the silent skeptics, active supporters have almost no influence. In the minds of the silent skeptics, the active supporters can't be trusted. Why? Because active supporters like *everything* and can do *anything (unlike the rest of us)*.

The target group for our communication should, in fact, be the silent skeptics. Communicating to this group can be a real challenge because we don't receive enough input or feedback from them to know where they stand. They rarely express their buy-in for the recommendation since they mainly sit on the fence. However, they are the group that, once involved, can most dramatically influence the success or failure of buy-in.

There are three keys for communicating to the silent skeptics. First, they hate to be "sold" on any change. They are very sensitive to being manipulated by others (even negativists, but especially management). It is important to present to them the full context for the solution, addressing how it fits into other changes, the recent history of trends in the organization, and it's general impact on the organization. Silent skeptics need understanding in order to feel comfortable with the change.

It is also important for silent skeptics to know exactly how they fit into the plans. They want to know as many specifics as possible about the ramifications of the solution on their roles, responsibilities and relationships in the workplace. Their main concern is for their security. This is probably the most challenging part of the communication since we can never provide them with as many details as they would like to have in order to feel comfortable.

Most importantly, we need to begin taking action as soon as possible. When that happens, any silent skeptics who are still sitting on the fence will go with the flow of others in order to avoid being made visible by their resistance. We know that the active supporters will be taking action on the change. So that leaves the negativists, who may be resisting the solution and not taking action. Unlike the silent skeptics, the negativists don't mind being visible about their resistance. Even if the negativists were to isolate themselves, so long as the active supporters and the silent skeptics are taking action, things can proceed. The influence of the negativists is highest *before* the solution is implemented, when it is still being discussed. Their strength lies in their ability to work on people's fears. They create illusions that the change will be a "catastrophe" before it happens.

Once actions are in motion, real results begin to replace the illusions created by the negativists. With proper tracking, we can establish a new norm or standard of behavior based on the implemented solutions and use that data to go back to the negativists to dispel their concerns and, more importantly, to offer them the opportunity to be part of the successful team. Most will prefer being on a winning team than to stand out as rebels without a cause. Not only does this strategy deal with the negativists, it also acknowledges the silent skeptics for their openness, participation and contribution to the success of the change.

For all these reasons, the sooner the solution is implemented, the better. It is only through action that people can alleviate concerns. The vast majority of fears will vanish as soon as people begin to deal with the realities of the change. When people are taking action, they're too busy focusing on getting the work done successfully to give much thought to whether or not they like the change. They're more likely to think of the change in terms of how they can implement it more effectively. That's healthy, productive thinking that will lead to concrete improvements in the way change is being implemented. It is fully appropriate to involve people in deciding how best to implement the solution, but not in whether the solution will take place, since that is a given. As problems arise, they will be addressed and dealt with because they are real, not theoretical. This

Rebels in the Pharmacy

A medical center had been involved with a series of changes for about four years and ran up against a department of rebels (the pharmacy department) which resisted every change. As the organization moved toward patient-centered care, more cross-functional problem solving teams, and greater accountability, the pharmacy department refused to participate in the change efforts. Several attempts to remedy this problem by involving the department in training sessions and communication efforts were made but did nothing to move the group toward a level of functioning consistent with the rest of the organization.

The problem was with the pharmacists themselves. They held the positional and educational power of the department and were unified as a group of negativists that intimidated everyone else, including management. The organization approached me to discuss the next intervention, which was to bring everyone together to discuss the problem one more time. Hearing this, I thought of the famous definition of insanity, "Doing the same thing over and over expecting a different result." We came up with a new strategy that involved an intervention workshop in which everyone in the department was required to participate. Naturally, many of the pharmacists didn't attend, and those who did either refused to participate or "bad-mouthed" the session. As a result, they were "excused" from attending. This left only the support staff which, although large in number, had previously had no voice in the department due to the influence of the pharmacists.

After the negativists left the session, it didn't take long for participation to increase. The support staff created strategies and agreements for making changes in the department. They developed ways to support each other amid the negativity of the pharmacists. Committed to taking action, they left the session empowered as a team and ready to make changes that they had always wanted to make, but had never had the opportunity to make without having to fear the consequences.

Within a few weeks, other departments were calling the pharmacy congratulating them for the major improvements in customer service, quality and responsiveness. By the time the pharmacists started complaining about how the changes would never work, the rest of the department had demonstrated a level of success that received public notice. Within four weeks, a four year old problem had been resolved, and a new norm of performance and behavior had been established within the pharmacy department.

The case was closed for good, and the pharmacists had a choice of whether or not to stay in the department. Interestingly enough, the most vocal negativists were those who later were to become the most cooperative, while some of the more silent ones eventually decided to leave. It isn't uncommon to find a few *silent* negativists who manage to provoke others to speak out and take the risks of resistance and rebellion.

requires, however, that more time be dedicated to evaluation and modification in order to refine the process as it evolves.

We must ask people to suspend judgment while the solution is being implemented. The *results* will create the buy-in, not in terms of people's opinion, but in terms of a concrete evaluation of how that change has affected the organization's desired outcomes and how effectively it has moved the organization in the clear direction articulated by senior management. In other words, the buy-in will be based on practical reasoning rather than on theory or opinions about the impending solution.

Create Understanding for a New Direction

As mentioned earlier, the term buy-in has always carried with it a notion of selling. Otherwise, why call it "buy" in? In the past, we've tried to "sell" the benefits of proposed change, instead of just presenting the full story. Most traditional organizations will say: *"We're going to implement a new solution to solve a problem and these are all the reasons why we should do it."* More sophisticated organizations might even present it in a slightly different manner: *"We're going to implement a solution, and to help you understand why, we need to examine the cost of our present situation. Look at all the negatives!"* Both approaches depend on a fundamentally dishonest manipulation of the facts since they don't reveal the whole story. This "sales oriented" approach creates skepticism, misunderstanding, and confusion about the solution once it is implemented. Often, people go through the motions of the change without really understanding why it is being made or even its intention.

Honest and open communication is at the core of an accountability-based® approach to communication. The truth is, *any* solution is going to have both advantages and drawbacks.

Presenting the context of the solution means presenting the pros and cons of the solution along with the pros and cons of the current situation. This better reflects the truth of the situation.

There are other, more tactical reasons why it is a mistake when communicating to talk only of the solution and ignore the current state. For one thing, we can't assume that people are already aware of the current state simply because they're living it. If it is not addressed, people will focus on how positive it is and ignore the problems that are presently an issue for the organization. Ironically, the same people who complain the loudest about all these problems in the organization will be the ones who will defend the status quo most adamantly once the solution or change is announced. Most people prefer the numbness of ignoring the current problems, and resist the "pain" associated with the proposed change.

There's an old story that if everyone took their troubles outside and placed them on their front lawns in order to have a neighborhood "troubles" exchange, everyone would choose their own troubles. Why? Familiar pain is always more tolerable than confronting an unfamiliar pain that we're not sure we can survive. So even though there may be more pain associated with the current situation than with the proposed situation, most people will still choose the familiar pain over the new pain.

This is where the communication strategy often falls apart. We tend to focus our strategy on emphasizing the benefits of the solution, when most people are worried about how the problems and pitfalls of the proposed solution will affect them. So they are much more motivated by the plans to solve the problems than they are by the plans to maximize the benefits. Therefore, what must be is a strategy and list of actions presented that deal with those "cons" of the proposed solution that can be influenced. We can ask for volunteers to participate in resolving any issues that don't have clear solutions. This call for participation elicits great support since we all have an interest in minimizing the pain associated with change. For instance, if we are moving to a team structure and don't yet have a method to compensate people for this new structure, how long would it take you to volunteer to participate on the committee responsible for figuring out the new compensation plan?

Presenting a strategy for minimizing the solution's cons and costs also reinforces management's credibility. People see that management is open about the drawbacks and have thought about solutions. We are likely to respond with cynicism and resistance to a change effort that is presented as a panacea. While our purpose may not be to attain buy-in in order to implement a solution, we do still want to elicit as much support for and participation in the change as possible, and we want to provide a means for people to take action immediately.

The more global the solution being introduced, the greater the need for presenting not only the current situation, but also the history of events leading up to the solution. This is accomplished by describing the external drivers along with the pros and cons of the organization as compared to its position five years ago, and what its new position will be after the proposed solution. The non-disputable factors are the external drivers of the past and current situation. It is easy to demonstrate that the organization needs to make changes that will respond to those external drivers. Then, a trend analysis can be created for those factors that will impact the organization in the upcoming five years. Based on these trends, we can predict the kinds of changes in the organization that will require our continued response, giving employees a deeper understanding of the change and the context needed for that change.

Finally, all managers presenting the solution to their teams must provide their teams with a clear choice about participating in the change. This is where the accountability is established. The importance of providing clear choices is well described by Kathleen Ryan and Daniel Oestreich in their book, *Driving Fear Out of the Workplace*, "Choice increases the positive experience with change. The greater the choice, the better the experience, even when the change leads to hours of hard work, the frustration of ambiguity, and the discipline required to develop new skills or knowledge. When choice is not present, people feel trapped; in extreme cases, they feel like victims."[2] While we don't often think this way, there are pros and cons to supporting the change as well as pros and cons to resisting the change.

Our role as managers is to respond to people's decision to support or resist new initiatives. Communicating the pros and cons of supporting or resisting a change lets employees know the consequences of their choice. For instance, some of the cons for supporting the solution may be that we will be making more mistakes. More conflicts may arise in the process of trying to meet customer needs. Some of the pros for resisting the change may be that we can continue doing things in the familiar way and we can stand out as the independent rebels in the group. However, the cons of resisting the change may include creating dissension and conflict within the team, and reducing our performance as a team, thus making it necessary for the manager to undertake more coaching and corrective action of non-performers. This is not a threat; it is a consequence which is then clearly articulated.

Too often, we refrain from stating the consequences which exist for unacceptable behavior or for a lack of performance. This

---

[2] Kathleen D. Ryan and Daniel K. Oestreich, *Driving Fear Out of the Workplace,* Jossey-Bass, Inc. Publishers.

results in a lack of accountability, a lack of boundaries, and the false impression that there *aren't* consequences. *The truth is that actions always have consequences, even if they are not clearly stated.* To pretend otherwise is to mislead people. I would rather managers be up-front about the consequences so that people can be aware of the ramifications of their choices. As is evident in the model below, stating (and carrying through with) real consequences provides people with the opportunity to adjust their thinking, learn from their mistakes, and make new choices. This is how people learn. If we don't provide consequences, people have to wait for extreme events to occur which bring on those consequences before they have a chance to learn. Then the cost can be very high.

Figure 8-1: Informed Choices

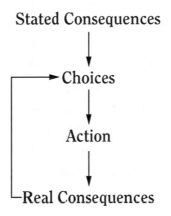

Applying this concept to my own home situation, I don't allow my eight year old daughter to play with a ball near the busy street in front of our house. If she does, I immediately tell her to go inside the house. She can choose to test me and receive the consequence, and then have the opportunity to make a new choice. My goal is to prevent the extreme consequence of her being run over by a car.

In organizations, we are not making people aware of the consequences of their choices. In cases of poor-performance, for example, we wait until our customers go elsewhere, which causes us to downsize our organization. By the time we downsize it's too late for people to make a new choice about their performance; they no longer have a job. The price is high when we lack an accountable work environment, one where expectations and consequences are clearly laid out.

Communication Must Be On-Going

While it is important to try to communicate the solution in such a way that everyone will become aware of the big picture, not everyone will "hear" the change in the same way, and not everyone will reach a point of understanding at the same time. Some people will have to see the solution take place before they will be able to understand the reason behind it. They will be able to understand it only in retrospect. However, it is still critical to communicate the context of the solution and to continue reinforcing and reiterating that context both during and after the initial implementation. Too often, leaders limit communication efforts to the period before the initial implementation begins. But people access information only when they are *ready* to do so, when they are no longer resistant to the ideas being presented, and when their experience helps to raise their consciousness to a point in which they can see things from a new perspective.

⮑ **9** ⮐

Strategy #4:
Execution—The Key
to High Performance

Myth: The purpose of team development is to improve relationships and morale.

Truth: The purpose of team development is to improve accountability and performance execution to achieve business outcomes.

As an 11 year old in sixth grade at a public school, I had one of my first team experiences outside of sports or music. Influenced by my grandfather, a practical joker, I devised an April Fool's joke to play on my teacher. It wasn't hard to convince two of my friends to go along with the gag. The plan was to hide ten significant items from our classroom, including the teacher's desk and other impressively large objects, so that when she walked in the empty room she would be shocked.

First, we planned the event. We identified which objects would disappear and the process for returning them. Because we had been studying poetry, we decided to present our teacher with rhyming clues to help her find each object. We also decided how we would decorate the room. We intended to have a party after she had successfully located all the missing items, and decided what food and drinks to have. In addition, we identified the key people whose support we required, including the principal. Not only did we need his permission, but also we needed him to let us in the room before school to hide everything and set up the decorations. Because of all the work involved, we decided to expand our committee by another five students.

We had so much fun. Everyone had a role and did their job on time even though it was a lot of work. We shared information effectively to maintain the necessary secrecy and to complete our tasks. We had a great plan and coordinated our activities smoothly. We didn't need to understand each other's style, though we used each other's strengths and interests to complete the various tasks. Although the prank had been my idea, we all participated in the leadership of this event. Everyone was aligned and there was no territorialism or fighting about who would take on certain tasks. We all cooperated as a team with a high level of trust even though we had never participated in any ropes courses or team building exercises. Our communication was effective even though we hadn't attended a course on communication. Even our classmates who weren't involved were supportive and kept their accountability by keeping it a secret.

As 11 year olds, we successfully designed, planned and implemented a fabulous April Fools event long before we understood the meaning of the words "design," "plan," and "implement." We had a clear purpose and participated fully. We counted on each other for support, guidance, effective communication, and for keeping our commitments. It was simple, painless and fun even though it required extra work and time. Everyone benefited from the experience—the "planning committee", the students, the teacher, and even the principal, who showed up for the party. Our accountability formed the backbone for our teamwork and our teamwork provided the backbone for our success.

Execution: The Missing Piece to Achieve Breakthrough Results

Before the introduction of the Quality Movement, high performance was achieved by building the skills of each individual in the organization. If a breakdown occurred, a person or group of people were "blamed" and then sent to a training program to gain skills in their area of deficiency. The assumption was that if everyone in the organization was highly skilled, we would have a high-performing organization.

Once the Quality Movement took hold, we changed our paradigm from blaming *people* to blaming the *processes*. At first we emphasized continuous improvement. Then, with the advancement toward re-engineering, we included the re-creation of processes in our improvement efforts. In both cases, we assumed that if operational processes were streamlined and employees were skilled, we would have a top performing organization. While streamlined processes and skilled employees are essential for effective performance, they are not enough to attain top performance.

Despite the time and effort spent implementing these programs, organizations still were not achieving the desired results on a consistent basis. In an effort to find out why, I examined high-performing organizations *outside* of the typical business environment.

When we watch a World Series baseball game, we are witnessing performances by the top baseball players in the country. They have the top skills to perform their job. They've been playing baseball for most of their lives and have used the same "plays" many times. When the batter hits the ball to the second baseman, the second baseman catches it and throws it to the first baseman to get the runner out. This is clearly the most streamlined play for getting the runner out.

When we watch the final championship game in the World Series, we witness two teams with the most streamlined plays performed by ballplayers who are the most skilled in their profession. Yet, even after an entire season, *they continue to practice in preparation for the final game.* They don't practice to increase skill and they don't practice to develop more stream-lined processes. Why, then, do they practice?

They practice to improve their "execution" of perfor-mance—to refine how they function as a team. The best ballplayers with the most streamlined processes still need to improve their linkages with each other. This involves improving their communication, fine-tuning their coordination and adjust-ing their timing in order to develop the highest performance possible. In addition, they practice "recovery" plays and decision making during crisis situations to prepare for the unexpected— like those times when the ball is dropped or when runners get on base. Ultimately, their execution is what determines how effec-tively they can avoid being scored against.

The same is true for a professional orchestra. All the musicians must be highly skilled—that goes without saying. They wouldn't have secured a job in a professional orchestra if they were not highly skilled. What they're practicing when they rehearse is how seamlessly they can perform together. Music critics often comment on precisely this ability when reviewing symphony concerts or recordings.

In organizations, we streamline our technical processes, but not our team processes. We fail to review the linkage and accountability among individuals and departments. This lack of focus on execution and recovery results in the breakdown of projects, the duplication of resources, and the existence of conflicting priorities between departments and/or people. At the same time, everyone is overwhelmed with too much information. Accountability breaks down not because of a lack of skills or technical processes, but because of a lack of team processes and tracking systems to ensure that linkages take place among the various performers.

Figure 9-1: High Performance.

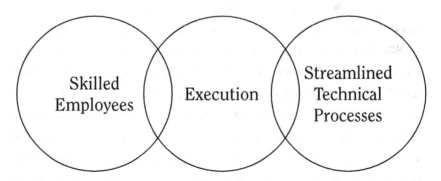

Execution is the link between people and technical processes which results in high performance.

Teams are the Vehicles for Effective Execution

Teams are the vehicles for applying the concepts and tools of execution to create an accountable culture and to achieve breakthrough results. James Kouzes and Barry Posner make a great case for this in their book, *The Leadership Challenge*, where they report, "In the more than 550 original cases that we studied, we didn't encounter a single example of extraordinary achievement that occurred without the active involvement and support of many people." They then add, "...People continue to tell us, 'You can't do it alone. It's a team effort.'"[1]

Unfortunately, most teams leave out the accountability factor. If they do any team development at all, it tends to focus around the different personality styles, general communication skills, awareness activities to emphasize the importance of teamwork, and visioning processes to create alignment. While these bits of knowledge are helpful as background, when the real work of a team needs to be accomplished—the work that involves sharing critical information, coordinating priorities, making decisions and managing conflicts—the team finds itself back in conflict, since they didn't work on these important aspects of performance execution and recovery, and have therefore undermined their own effectiveness.

Recently I received a phone call from a Boston-based client who wanted to tell me about the latest improvement program being piloted in her organization. "We're piloting the use of teams in our organization to determine if it will work in our culture," she said. This organization was a highly technical research-oriented institution that relied on the sharing of infor-

---

[1] James M. Kouzes and Barry Z. Posner, *The Leadership Challenge: How to Keep Getting Extraordinary Things Done in Organizations*, Jossey-Bass Publishers, 1995.

mation, the coordination of projects, and the utilization of limited resources. To ask the question of whether or not teams would work in this culture was to miss the point.

In most organizations, teamwork is not an option. It already exists. As long as two or more people are sharing information, making decisions, or coordinating activities, teamwork is already in place. Whether it is effective or not is another story. These are the issues of execution that need to be "practiced" to become effective. If the organization is managing projects and establishing agreements to build trust, then it is also necessary to add recovery systems to be prepared for the unexpected. Peter Senge emphasizes the importance and value of teams in his book, *The Fifth Discipline*. "Team learning is vital because teams, not individuals, are the fundamental learning unit in modern organizations. This is where the 'rubber meets the road.'"[2] Without having teams focus on how they execute and recover, the team ends up dysfunctional and slow to re-spond—just as any athletic team or music group would be if they decided not to practice. When teams do review and upgrade their execution and recovery, high performance and break-through results become the outcome. As Senge reminds us, "When teams are truly learning, not only are they producing extraordinary results, but the individual members are growing more rapidly than could have occurred otherwise."

Teams provide the mechanism for creating true accountability—an environment in which people can count on each other for their performance and positive relationships. This goes beyond the hierarchical form of accountability where employees are accountable only to their bosses. In a true team, members are also accountable to one another. But most organizations aren't

---

[2] Peter M. Senge, *The Fifth Discipline,* Currency Doubleday, 1990.

structured to support the teamwork necessary for effective performance, nor do they have the processes in place to ensure that the teamwork that *does* exist results in bottom-line results.

The Misuse of Teams

Some improvement programs drift in and out of popularity. Teams have been popular during the past ten years. They were also popular about thirty years ago. Like many improvement programs that enjoy popular appeal, teams are often *mis*used by organizations. In some cases this misuse is destructive; in others, it is merely counterproductive.

Teams have been used by managers as a way to avoid coaching or disciplining the non-performers. They use the "team process" to mobilize coworkers to deal with a non-performer on the team. The result is that no one deals with the non-performer and now the entire team resents the manager for avoiding his own responsibility and for creating more work.

Teams are sometimes called "committees," "task forces" or "project teams." We all know of at least one organization which, anxious to make a change without taking on the responsibility for communicating the "bad news," decided to "empower" employees to form a committee that would study the problem, make a recommendation and implement a change. Then the employees could be blamed for the change rather than management. Naturally, this type of manipulation undermines trust.

Another misuse of teams is as a vehicle to eliminate an entire management level by "empowering" a team of employees to manage themselves. Initially, the team will probably welcome its new autonomy. But rarely is the autonomy provided with a clear direction or with coaching. Later, the team finds it has no representation in the organization for getting more resources or for being developed for advancement opportunities. In short, their "gift" of autonomy comes with the seeds of self-destruction.

Teams can be misused inadvertently. This occurs when an organization creates teams from individuals who share no common purpose and who function autonomously. Such "forced-upon" teamwork leads to confusion, animosity among team members and territorialism, with everyone scurrying to protect his or her own "turf" in the process of team development.

When organizations use teams to build morale, improve relationships, empower employees, or transfer accountability from managers to employees, the results are usually short-term at best. While teams can produce these kinds of positive results, making this their sole purpose can backfire, as was the case with a large governmental agency that wanted to build greater trust and communication within its management team. In an effort to create a team environment, they participated in ropes courses, style assessments, team building sessions, and other activities. After two years, their relationships with one another had improved, but their team functioning hadn't changed. They still weren't accomplishing their goals as a team and they were still fighting each other for resources. Teams are only a means to an end, not an end in and of themselves.

What Kind of Team is Most Appropriate?

Recently I worked with the senior management team of the Santa Clara Welfare Agency in California. They recognized the need to create more of a team structure within their organization in order to increase accountability, share resources more effectively and improve performance. However, they became stuck when a team member asked, "How do we know what kind of teams we should have? Should we be like a track team where everyone has his or her own event but practices on the same field? Or should we be like a football team, where we coordinate each play with one another?" As a philosophy, there is no simple answer to that question. In practice, however, we can answer it by examining the organization's desired business outcomes, specifically, the priorities and projects associated with outcomes. First we must identify all of the functional areas and individuals who are either affected by each priority project or are needed for support in order to successfully complete the priority project. Then, based on those identified interdependencies, teams can be created in such a way as to ensure that everyone involved with the success of the project is involved with each other and accountable to each other to ensure successful results.

A formalized team doesn't mean a structured and fixed team. It means a fluid team, much like an orchestra, where members function together as needed and in an efficient and well-coordinated manner. All the instruments don't necessarily play together at the same time, but instead contribute to the piece at different times. A baseball team provides another model. For example, only a part of the infield is involved when a double play is made, even though other members of the team are there as backup.

To return to the question posed by the team member at the Welfare Agency, the decision about *what type of team to form* is less important than the exercise of determining *the necessary interdependencies among the team members* for achieving their priorities. As illustrated in Figure 9-2, some priorities will require a higher degree of teamwork and interdependence than others will. An organization with a higher level of interdependence also will require a higher level of accountability as outlined in the Accountability Continuum in Chapter 1.

Figure 9-2: Priority Matrix indicating degree of Cross-Functional Teamwork.

Department Priorities	Finance	Training	Mktg.	Sales	Dist.	Admin.
1	✓		✓		✓	
2	✓	✓	✓			
3	✓	✓	✓	✓	✓	✓
4			✓	✓	✓	
5		✓		✓		✓
6	✓	✓	✓			
7		✓				✓
8	✓					
9	✓		✓	✓	✓	✓
10	✓	✓	✓		✓	✓

For this department, Priority #3 will require more teamwork than Priority #7.

Recovery: The Secret of High-Performing Execution

What do top-performing baseball teams focus on when they practice? Recovery. The coach sets up "what if" scenarios in which the team must deal with the unexpected. What happens when things break down? What happens when the infielder misses the ball, the pitcher gets tired, or runners get on base due to a problem with the playing field? The coach makes sure that the team practices its ability to recover when various crises occur. Everyone develops the skills to respond to difficult situations, as well as the ability to mobilize the team to recover from the breakdown in the most effective manner.

Dr. Benjamin Carson employs a similar principle in his operating room. A legend in the medical community, he was named Chief of Pediatric Neurosurgery at Johns Hopkins Hospital in Baltimore in 1984, at the age of 33 becoming the youngest U.S. doctor ever to hold such a position. Three years later he made history by leading the first successful operation to separate Siamese twins joined at the head. Today, he performs up to 500 operations annually, which is double the caseload of most neurosurgeons. One of the ways he handles the pressure is by playing classical music in the operating room. Another way is by planning for problems. "[I] focus clearly on what can go wrong," he says. "I think through every procedure; how I expect it to go, how long each phase will last, when I can move on to the next one. But the real value of planning comes when things don't go the way I expect. I always anticipate the worst-case scenario: What's the worst thing that could happen? What can I do to make sure it doesn't? What will I do if it does?"

Contingency plans in organizations are rarely given the attention they deserve. Project planning meetings will address the project outcome, the benefits, the strategy and the action plan and still somehow miss identifying the potential breakdowns. Too often when a breakdown occurs, people are caught off-guard. They panic, sometimes fleeing from the situation, creating yet another problem that begins to snowball.

Generally, the team with the fastest and most effective recovery will be the highest performing team. Its members can respond to both crisis situations and to changes most effectively, since they are best equipped with the flexibility and responsiveness required to continually adjust according to the "external drivers" of the situation. No problem is too great for the team that knows how to recover quickly. In the book, *Corporate Lifecycles: How and Why Corporations Grow and Die and What to Do About It,*" Ichak Adizes describes the difference between "young" and "old" organizations. He says, "Young means the organization can change relatively easily, although what it will do because it has a low level of control is fairly unpredictable. 'Old' means there is controllable behavior, but the organization is inflexible; it has little propensity to change."[3] Developing recovery systems enables the organization to be both flexible and controllable making it neither too young nor too old.

These are skills that can not only be learned, but practiced. By focusing on recovery during team development sessions, teams can work out the "plays" ahead of time. Each member of the team will know how to coordinate efforts, use resources, and communicate effectively (by sharing only pertinent information), and will trust that the other members of the team will carry out their predetermined roles and functions. This goes far beyond the standard fare of most team-building workshops. This is where we practice how we function together as a team in order to achieve the highest levels of execution and recovery, since in order to perform as an organization we need to depend on each other and have the proper linkages in place. As the team members change, the priorities change or the roles of the team members change, and so new processes for execution and recovery must be created to adapt to the new situation. Similarly, athletic teams and music groups must change their strategy of performance based on the new talent that comes into the group.

---

[3] Ichak Adizes, *Corporate Lifecycles: How and Why Corporations Grow and Die and What to Do About It,* Prentice Hall, 1988.

The Five Stages of Recovery

When a problem surfaces, recovery can either be a seamless operation of awareness and response, or a dragged out process of hiding and blame. To create enough "safety" for people to admit mistakes, raise concerns, and hold others accountable, it is useful to understand the five primary stages of recovery.

Figure 9-3: The Five Stages of Recovery

STAGE	TITLE	DESCRIPTION
I (FASTEST)	Self-Correction	We look for, find, and resolve our own mistakes.
II	Observation by Co-worker	Co-worker points out a problem with our performance and we self-correct.
III	Coaching by Co-worker	Co-worker points out a problem and assists us in improving our performance.
IV	Coaching by Manager	Manager points out a problem and assists us in improving our performance.
V (SLOWEST)	Corrective Action by Manager	After coaching has failed, manager implements corrective action process to either improve performance or to find a new team player who will perform.

Stage I: Self-Correction

We've already seen how the team with the fastest recovery will be the highest performing team. So, specifically, what can we do to improve our recovery time? First, we have to become aware that a problem exists. The sooner we realize that a problem exists, the faster we can recover from it. The fastest way to do that is for each of us to be aware of our own mistakes as soon as they occur. This takes commitment from each person to a level of personal excellence that keeps them looking for opportunities for improvement. This description embodies the role of "change activist" discussed earlier in Chapter 5. While self-correction is desired, it is humanly impossible for us to always recover at Stage I.

Unfortunately, we can't always see when we're making a mistake, or when we're not performing optimally. Maybe the clarinet player in the orchestra plays a B-natural instead of a B-flat in bar 135, realizes it, and corrects himself the next time the passage is performed. But suppose it is a very atonal piece, hence his "ear" is no longer recognizing the misplayed note as incorrect. What then?

Stage II: Observation by Co-Worker

The next fastest route to recovery is to have a team member observe and point out the problem to the person who is responsible for it. The conversation in the clarinet section might go something like this.

"How come you're playing a B-natural in bar 135?"

" That's what's written."

"No. It's a B-flat. Look!"

"That's amazing! You're right. The first time that passage comes up it's a B-natural, but here it's a B-flat. How could I have missed that!?"

And you can be sure he won't miss it the next time.

Too often, though, what happens in organizations with vertical accountability is that team members are reluctant to point out errors to one another for fear of hurting egos or seeming disloyal. There is no "safety" for doing so. Instead, team members cover for one another, and perhaps grumble about it privately. It is safer to provide support for our teammates who make a mistake than it is to criticize them.

Stage III: Coaching by Co-Worker

Sometimes the person whose performance is less than optimal does not know how to recover on his own. In an accountability-based® organization, a member of that person's team will offer to provide some coaching. Maybe the clarinet player isn't just playing a wrong note. Maybe that piece contains a highly complex rhythmical pattern that he just doesn't "get", and consequently he keeps missing his cue which throws off the second clarinet player sitting next to him. In this scenario, the second clarinet player might offer to work with him on that passage or give him a tip that will help him. Again, many organizations are not set up for this type of coaching which instead is often viewed as "interfering." Without a safe environment for this type of feedback and coaching among team members to occur, the team's performance will rarely be optimal, no matter how much people like, trust, and respect one another.

Stage IV: Coaching by Manager

Sometimes team members don't cooperate with one another either in their linkage or in their own individual performance. At other times, they just aren't in a position to learn from one another. Their styles may be different. In this case it is necessary for the manager to step in and provide direct coaching. The manager offers his or her perspective, skill, encouragement, and the articulation of clear expectations and deadlines. This is where recovery begins in many organizations.

Stage V: Corrective Action by Manager

If the problem continues, the leader needs to move into corrective action with the specific non-performing team member to ensure that his or her performance improves and that he becomes a contributing team member. This corrective action process involves documentation as well as contact with the human resources specialist in order to ensure fairness both to the employee as well as to the employee's co-workers.

Low Performance
and the Breakdown of Recovery

I'll never forget an experience I had working with an architecture design company's small executive team consisting of a CEO and his five vice-presidents. During interviews which occurred before our intervention, the CEO complained that his vice-presidents didn't take enough initiative and that their follow-up was weak. The vice-presidents, in turn, complained that the CEO didn't give up authority. During our intervention, I introduced a non-work related activity (assembling a puzzle) to see how they would function together. Each person was given one piece of the puzzle and the team had to fit the pieces together to form the puzzle within three minutes, and without talking to one another. When the exercise began, each member of the team passed the first test by giving up their piece of the puzzle to the rest of the team in order to allow everyone to move all the pieces. Each member, including the CEO, passed the second test by managing to come up with different options to form the puzzle but without dominating the team. However, they still weren't successful in putting the puzzle together. I then announced that there was only one minute left so that I could see how they would react under pressure.

Suddenly, upon that announcement, the CEO stood up and pulled all the pieces of the puzzle in front of him. For the next 45 seconds, the CEO worked by himself to put the puzzle together, while the vice-presidents watched. Finally, one of the vice-presidents stood up, went over to the CEO, and leaned over him to shift the pieces of the puzzle together to complete the puzzle.

We all laughed at how this activity closely reflected the way in which this team functioned in the workplace. So often, managers are more comfortable trying to solve all the problems that exist rather then coaching and developing others to solve problems for themselves, allowing them to increase their own effectiveness as leaders.

Most organizations aren't set up to initiate recovery before reaching Stage IV, the stage at which the manager must become involved. Can you imagine an athletic team or music group that had to wait for the coach or director to find and surface every performance problem on the team? They would no longer be top performing, that's for sure.

Even when the problem involves the entire team, people are still reluctant to bring up the issue for resolution. So everyone pretends it doesn't exist until the manager raises the issue or until it becomes the topic of discussion for a "task force" focused on the next quality improvement program. So long as organizations support a system of vertical accountability, they will not provide the safety for co-workers to support each other by raising issues for the purpose of resolving them.

Many managers, even, are reluctant to provide the necessary guidance. Some have abdicated their role under the guise of "empowering the employee to improve", while others avoid the discomfort by giving poor performers a satisfactory score on their performance review as long as they promise to do better next time. Several years later, when they haven't improved, they are transferred to another department where the process repeats itself.

When a leader fails to deal with a performance problem, everyone loses. The poor performer never improves, which ultimately catches up with him—possibly in the next downsizing. Additionally, his high-performing teammates must increase their own efforts in order to maintain an effective operation. But even they cannot cover for a weak teammate indefinitely. Anyone can have a bad day, and other team members must be prepared and equipped to accommodate those bad days. But when one team member is chronically having bad days, no room is left for other team members to have their bad days. Ultimately, the high-performing team members will break down in their efforts to make up for the chronically poor performance of their teammate. Likewise, the team's approach becomes less than optimal because it *has* to compensate for a weak link. This is like jogging with a limp—after a while the good leg collapses under the added strain. The team experiences stress, burnout, and eventually dysfunctional performance, ultimately leading to self-doubt. Ironically, it is at this very point that leaders often implement a team-building effort to try to solve the problem, though their avoidance of their own leadership role as coach to the non-performer continues.

Instead of running away from performance problems, we need to address them as quickly as possible. The faster we address a problem, whether it involves a technical process, team process, an individual's performance, or some other problem, the less painful it is for everyone.

The System to Develop a High Performance Team

High-performing teams are not created or developed through any kind of event like ropes courses, retreats, or other similar "bonding" activities. High-performing teams are developed over time by improving the team's execution. This can be achieved through a five-step process which develops for the team a unified, clear direction, establishes clear priorities and measurements for success, contains a built-in system to review milestones that ensure progress, and has systems to continually improve linkages between team members such that high performance and responsive execution is reached.

Step 1: Lay Out the Intention

The place to start is with a microcosm of the intention statement that was discussed in Chapter 6. The team must develop its own mission and values as well as identify the external factors both within and outside of the organization. The intention should be updated regularly to provide increasing levels of clarity as the team learns what it needs to do to ensure accomplishment of the mission and respond to external drivers. Generally, the meaning behind the stated intention becomes more detailed, more comprehensive and clearer as the team approaches the fulfillment of that intention. It describes in narrative form the dynamics of what people are doing and how they are doing it in order to reach the level of quality, innovation, customer service and responsiveness required to perform efficiently. An intention statement not only lets people know what needs to be achieved, but gives them a picture of how it will actually look in terms of culture and operational linkages.

Intention for Office Operations Department

The office support staff work as an integrated team, similar to a baseball team. Each team member plays his or her own position; however, any team member can cover for the other team members. Team members expand their flexibility in the office as a part of their personal development, while increasing technical knowledge to keep up with changing demands from clients and competitors.

As a high functioning team, each person handles a multitude of projects at once and has the ability to prioritize the projects according to the critical needs and time frames of our customers. As priorities shift, the team mobilizes its strengths to the changing needs, optimizing activities to complete the tasks in the most efficient manner possible. This is what energizes the team. When projects are less dynamic, the support team strategically plans the project, milestones, and activities to optimize their efficiency. They are in constant communication with the involved or affected customer(s) to coordinate and update the progress of the project. Project plans always consider the overall purpose of the assignment, how it fits into a more global effort, and the timing that is involved. Plans are shared with all involved parties to ensure buy-in and completeness before, during and after plans are finalized. Even the smallest task is sized up and integrated with other current priorities before committing to a time frame.

When it comes to completing a project, all team members both inside and outside of the office are accountable for their parts of the project in a timely manner according to a mutually agreed upon process plan and schedule. Quality is checked as a routine part of the output, both during and after the process. Team members use each other cross-functionally to check each other's work. Changes to the schedule and problems are communicated immediately to the affected team members, and adjustments are made to optimize the completion of the project. Updating others on the status of projects or notifying others of upcoming projects or assignments takes place in time to allow others to prepare for the events even before the clarity of the project or assignment can be communicated. In other words, don't wait to warn others of a tidal wave. Our effective coordination is a reflection of our highest respect and regard for each other's time and effort.

The office staff meets on a regular basis to review workloads, priorities, and process improvement. During these meetings, the team works on the improvement of processes, skills and functioning between team members.

The atmosphere in the office is enthusiastic, energetic, professional, relaxed and confident. Customers feel comfortable in the working environment, and view the team as highly professional and a model of teamwork. Each member challenges the others to their highest level of performance. It is a fun team to be a part of due to its continual success, and is respected as a model support staff team.

If you were on this office operations team, you'd know what was expected, how you fit in with the other team members and what excellent customer service looked like. More importantly, you would know how all these aspects of your job were integrated. Within six months of creating this intention, the office operations department improved its level of functioning and quality significantly, as well as its relationship with internal and external customers.

Step 2: Develop Success Factors

Once the intention is clear, the team can begin to identify a list of success factors which describe in detail everything that the team will be doing in the context of fulfilling its intention. Success Factors are created by answering the question, "If you are already accomplishing your intention at the highest level of excellence imaginable, what will it look, sound, and feel like on your team?"

Success factors are expressed in terms of statements that describe specific behaviors that affect things such as performance and culture. They may include characteristics such as efficiency, customer service, professionalism, training, safety, quality, documentation, communication, cross-functional relationships, teamwork, morale, and leadership.

Success Factors are *not* goals. Goals are temporary while Success Factors are longer term. In a sense, Success Factors represent the "Blueprint" for success of an organization or team. It is a set of criteria by which the organization or team must function to achieve its desired outcomes. It becomes the "positive focus" for the organization or team. In John-Roger's book, *Spiritual Warrior*, he makes the distinction between positive thinking and positive focus. "With positive thinking, we can be drowning but telling ourselves that things are just great. With positive focus we tell ourselves things will be great—as soon as we get to shore. Then we focus on the shore and get moving."[4] Success Factors are one of the most important elements in turning an intention into a reality.

It takes most teams less than two hours to come up with between 25 and 35 different success factors representing all aspects of performance execution and effective team relation-

---

[4] John-Roger, *Spiritual Warrior: The Art of Spiritual Living,* Mandeville Press, 1998.

Samples of Success Factors from the Operation Team

1. Scheduling changes that arise are quickly and effectively communicated to others who may be affected by the change.

2. Our work areas are orderly and free of clutter so that even those unfamiliar with our work area can easily find what they need.

3. All projects are logged onto the job board upon receipt, and we immediately review the scheduling for conflicts and reprioritize jobs as necessary for maximum work flow and minimum crisis.

4. We stay well educated on leading-edge technologies and techniques by attending classes and seminars, by acquiring and studying texts, and by subscribing to and reading a broad range of technical magazines and periodicals.

5. We proactively pursue input and feedback from consultants and clients, and we regard any unsolicited opinions they may offer as constructive criticism and an opportunity for improvement.

6. We effectively manage our own time to meet our customers' needs and exceed their expectations.

7. We embrace challenges with a "How Can We?" approach, rather than a binary "Can/Can't" or an "Either/Or" approach.

8. We conduct thorough research and make recommendation for the hardware and software necessary to ensure that our customers' needs are met with minimal frustration and crisis.

9. Even when our processes are working efficiently, we are continually looking for methods of improvement.

10. We cost-effectively utilize the finest raw materials and technologies to design and produce training, promotional, and exhibition materials of the highest quality available.

11. Each of us regards personal growth and improvement as the core of our organizational, team, and individual success; and in that spirit, we openly turn to others to both request and offer coaching and support.

---

ships. As a blueprint for success, it is time well spent. Success Factors are developed to include statements that embrace two extremes necessary for excellence that represent the "Genius of the And" as described by James Collins and Jerry Porras in their book, *Built to Last.*[5]

A team's success factors provide clear direction and clear standards. They can be used in hiring and orienting new team members and coaching existing ones when individual performance is not in alignment with the team's performance. Success factors can be measured for effectiveness and used as a foundation for identifying team improvement goals. Like the intention statement, success factors should be updated on a regular basis to provide greater clarity and understanding.

Step 3: Identify Priorities

Because of the continuous changes within organizations and the complex interdependencies that arise in order to accommodate those changes, it is critical that teams have a process for clarifying priorities and expectations. One of the key reasons so many teams feel overwhelmed is that new priorities are continually added to their plate while old ones are never eliminated. It is not uncommon for a team to face the impossible goal of accomplishing 25-30 priorities within a six-month period. What happens is that each week the team addresses a different priority, based on the crisis of the week. Eventually, everyone becomes aware that little progress has been achieved on any of the priorities because of the team's fragmentation. So once again a lot of effort is expended, producing little result.

It would be far more effective for a team to take one hour every three to five months for the purpose of identifying its top priorities for the next few months. At the same time a regular

---

[5] James C. Collins and Jerry I. Porras, *Built to Last: Successful Habits of Visionary Companies,* Harper & Row, 1997.

meeting structure would be established for monitoring progress, surfacing and solving breakdowns, making decisions, and taking action. Instead of focusing on sharing information, this kind of meeting is focused on action and results. This saves an enormous amount of wasted effort and ensures that the team is accomplishing the highest priorities.

In traditional organizations, the manager assigns priorities, which the employees carry out, and then everyone gets together and gives progress reports. But conflicting priorities are never dealt with in advance because the interconnectedness of everyone's individual activities and priorities is never examined. In an accountability-based® organization, the cross-functional interdependence is identified immediately so that the proper linkages and accountability can be established.

Step 4: Create a Priority Matrix

The team's priorities, of course, exist independently of those of the individual members of the team. Therefore, it is critical for each team member to identify his or her own top six to ten priorities, as well as those of the team members affected by those priorities. The team members required to assist in the meeting for discussing these priorities must also be identified. This information is used to create a Priority Matrix, which shows, at a glance, how the interlocking pieces fit together. Each team member shares his or her priority matrix with the others so that their interdependencies can be reviewed.

Conflicting priorities will be discovered, omissions of key individuals will surface, and miscoordination will be identified. Once these problems are solved, expectations are created between team members in terms of actions to be taken, decisions to be made, and the timing of activities. Then, if priorities do change, the matrix provides an easy means for letting others know of these changes so that they can adapt their expectations and involvement level accordingly. Below is an example of a Priority Matrix for a human resource department of a mid-sized company.

Figure 9-4: Sample Priority Matrix for a Human Resource department

Department Priorities	Compensation	Training	Personnel	Organizational Development
1. Creating an Accountable Culture	✓	✓	✓	✓
2. Improving the Performance Appraisal System		✓	✓	✓
3. Modifying the New Employee Handbook			✓	
4. Redesigning New Employee Orientation		✓	✓	
5. Reviewing the 401K Plan	✓			

Step 5: Interlocking Accountability— The Key Ingredient for Quick Recovery

In the past we blamed the traditional hierarchy for preventing organizations from performing effectively. We tried to develop more effective organizational structures, such as matrix organizations, flat organizations, or business unit organizations. However, after restructuring, people would still function in their territorial and controlling posture. The problem is not with the hierarchical structure. The problem is with the way we operate within the structure—how we've defined the "ground rules" for functioning level to level, department to department, and individual to individual. We define the functioning of the hierarchy in terms of vertical accountability, where a person is accountable to a boss who is accountable to another boss. Unfortunately, vertical accountability by itself can never be optimal because it limits accountability to the next manager or leader in the hierarchy. Rarely does it allow for accountability to the people whom we really affect—our co-workers. See Figure 9-5, *The Interlocking Accountability Model*.

On any high-performing athletic team or music group, team members are accountable to each other. It doesn't matter whether they are at different pay levels or at different levels of seniority, they are accountable for setting and keeping agreements, for supporting one another, for holding each other accountable when agreements aren't kept, and for challenging one another to strive towards their next level of successful performance. This doesn't replace the leader's role; rather, it functions *in addition* to vertical accountability. It is effective in a hierarchical organization or a matrix organization or a business unit. We call it "interlocking accountability," which means that we are accountable to everyone on whom we have an impact regardless of their position, level, or function.

Interlocking accountability demands that we are accountable for our performance and relationships *and for holding each other accountable when agreements are broken or a breakdown occurs*. In most organizations, people either 1) ignore the person responsible for the breakdown, and talk behind his back to every other team member hoping that he'll get the message without knowing who has sent it; or 2) blame the person for being a bad team member. Both cases promote victimization and separation rather than teamwork.

Figure 9-5: Interlocking Accountability

Each team member is accountable
to all affected team members
for his or her relationships, performance, and agreements.

Each team member is accountable
for holding other team members accountable
for either breaking an agreement or keeping an agreement using:

ACKNOWLEDGEMENT
(without judgement)
and
SUPPORT.

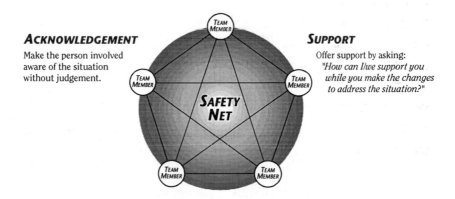

ACKNOWLEDGEMENT

Make the person involved
aware of the situation
without judgement.

SUPPORT

Offer support by asking:
"How can I/we support you
while you make the changes
to address the situation?"

Each person acknowledges and supports the other team members,
both when they are successful and when an agreement is broken.

Interlocking accountability functions through acknowledgment and support. If a breakdown occurs, we acknowledge it without judgment, and offer assistance to the person responsible, without actually solving the breakdown for him. Warren Bennis and Burt Nanus refer to acknowledging people without judgment as one of the key skills of leadership in their book, *Leaders: The Strategies for Taking Charge,* "The ability to accept people as they are, not as you would like them to be. In a way, this can be seen as the height of wisdom—to 'enter the skin' of someone else, to understand what other people are like on *their* terms, rather than judging them."[6] When we greet mistakes with acknowledgment and support rather than blame and punishment, we have the safety and accountability to continually work on improving performance, and to deal with crises head on.

In short, the new paradigm maximizes performance by increasing the speed and effectiveness with which a team recovers when things go wrong. They don't have to wait for the manager to become involved for the recovery process to begin.

Step 6: Develop Interaction Agreements

To ensure that performance isn't interrupted by relationship issues such as unresolved conflict, miscommunication and a lack of trust, high-performing teams create their own interaction agreements. These solidify the practical operational relationships among people, functions, and departments. They determine how conflicts will be resolved. They represent how team members will work together in *all* aspects of their functioning. These include agreements regarding how information will be shared, how team members will be supported by one another, how decisions will be made, and how trust will be maintained. Interaction agreements are NOT just guidelines for behavior. The tendency is to abort the guidelines when the behaviors are less than perfect. Interaction

[6] Warren Bennis and Burt Nanus, *Leaders: The Strategies for Taking Charge,* Harper & Row Publishers, Inc., 1985.

agreements include a set of conditions for acceptance that incorporates all the behaviors associated with keeping an agreement. The conditions also include recovery systems for the times when an agreement is broken.

While it may take a couple of hours for a team to hammer out several solid interaction agreements, it will save hundreds of hours of time spent later in stifled processes or unproductive meetings stemming from unresolved conflicts, a rehashing of issues, incomplete tasks for important projects, or lack of participation.

Interaction agreements provide the process for reinforcing interlocking accountability. In order to remain effective, interaction agreements must be reviewed at team meetings on a regular basis to ensure consistency and accountability. If people are failing to keep their agreements, they are held accountable with acknowledgment and support consistent with their recovery process and in a manner that encourages team alignment and unity. Agreements that have been kept should also be acknowledged to support the team members in their improvement efforts. Sometimes, upon review, an agreement must be changed for practical reasons or because the team isn't ready to demonstrate the level of trust required by the agreement. Since this process is an evolutionary one, interaction agreements must be revised over time. It is not uncommon to witness a team increasing their levels of trust 50 to 75 percent within a six to twelve month period through the use of interaction agreements.

Ultimately, the goal is to create teams in which members have the safety to challenge each other in a supportive way and to surface and resolve conflict without getting stuck in hurt feelings. When that is possible, no crisis or change is too great for the team to handle, once they know how to recover with grace, speed, and a unified focus. See Figure 9-6.

Figure 9-6: Interaction Agreement Example

GUIDELINE:

1. *Each team member will freely express his/her opinions and feelings along with the explanation for those opinions/feelings during team discussions.*

CONDITIONS FOR ACCEPTANCE:

a) *People will ask questions to better understand your position, rather than ask questions to make you wrong or put you on the defensive.*

b) *No retribution from anyone on the team.*

c) *No holding a grudge.*

d) *Don't share humor at the expense of respecting each individual or their ideas.*

e) *If you feel put down, or aren't sure of people's intentions, raise the issue.*

f) *Focus on issues, not the person; disagree with respect.*

g) *Demonstrate understanding for another person's point of view before disagreeing.*

h) *Don't act on assumptions; ask questions or check out your assumption.*

i) *No attacking of others or their programs.*

j) *Don't over-talk the needs/problems within your dept. or go on tangents.*

k) *Don't speak for someone else's position.*

l) *Don't line up votes or lobby outside of the meeting related to Leadership Team issues.*

m) *If you feel someone is over-talking or on a tangent or that lobbying has taken place, bring it up to the team for direction.*

n) *If someone is approaching you to lobby a vote, remind them of the agreement.*

Win-Win Interaction Agreements

Information Systems and Technology (IS&T) for the University of California, Berkeley was structured into five separate areas. Each area performed autonomously, and within each area, individuals were also very autonomous. At the same time, their customers regularly complained that they were out of touch. They didn't share information when problems occurred, and they had major malfunctions during times of transition.

This department developed a clear intention for effective performance along with a set of success factors that identified the functional behaviors necessary for success. They also established a set of interaction agreements for ensuring their ability to resolve conflicts, to make decisions and to coordinate the sharing of information and resources.

After six months and an improvement of 83% on their success factors, they also received glowing reports from their customers. There were no quality breakdowns, more problem solving taking place with customers directly, an increase in cross-functional problem solving, and a large reduction in costs. Not only was the team performing at higher levels of quality and efficiency with fewer staff (due to outside influences), but also the morale in the department had increased significantly.

The team members were unanimous in their response to the question of what contributed most significantly to their success: "We now have a recovery plan both for our projects and for our relationships. If anything goes wrong, it doesn't cause a crisis, it just mobilizes us to respond in a planned way to get results despite problems. We work better together, assisting and coaching one another, and we achieve greater results at the same time. Everyone wins!"

∽ **10** ∽

Strategy #5:
Develop Employees to be
Accountable High Performers

Myth: Training is successful when the employee
has demonstrated desired skills and
competencies.

Truth: Training is successful when the employee
has achieved his or her desired business
outcomes.

John hadn't been performing for several years, when I inherited him two years ago," the manager of an information systems department told me. "Since then, I made sure that he attended a series of workshops both at our organization and at the local college to upgrade his skills."

"Has his performance improved?" I asked.

"No!"

It turned out that the manager had never stated any expectations of John in terms of using his workshop experience and skills to improve his performance on the job. His only directive was for John to build his skills by taking a series of workshops.

How many times are people sent on training programs without expectations tied to their performance on the job? In fact, how often have you seen training programs tied to performance at all? Usually, the assessment of training is based on evaluations at the end of the workshop, and these focus on people's attitudes to the training program. We read comments like, "Best program I ever went to…I learned a lot!" or "I didn't like the program because it was too long."

The value of such courses must extend beyond awareness and skills to *actions* that contribute to higher levels of job performance. If a course is given on safety in the workplace, then we should expect safety records to show an improvement, or if already excellent, for that level to be sustained. If a course is given in management, there should be indicators that demonstrate better leadership and management effectiveness as a result of the course. Where do we get those indicators, especially for a subject like leadership or communication? How do we measure the impact?

The Breakdown of Traditional Assessments

Needs assessment is probably the most established form of assessment. It is usually developed using a survey of "needs" that is completed by managers and employees. Unfortunately, needs assessments generally reflect what managers and employees *want* for training rather than what they *need*. For example, in many organizations the need for "better communication" or for "dealing with conflict" are identified by needs assessments year after year, despite the fact that workshops are given on those subjects every year.

Even if the needs assessment reflects needs instead of wants, it generally reflects the needs of the past six months, since that is the natural reference point for people completing the assessment. By the time the organization responds to the stated needs with the appropriate workshops or interventions, the data is already dated by a year or more. In today's fast-paced, changing environment, this response is too late.

Aptitude assessment, popularized some time ago, is designed to identify the ideal aptitude for a particular job or role in the organization. Each employee takes an aptitude test to see how well he or she matches the ideal picture. Then they take skill-building programs to address any weaknesses that the tests reveal. This approach assumes that aptitude relates to action, which is rarely the case. It also assumes that the aptitude for any particular role will remain static.

More recently, the use of competency based assessments has become popular. These assessments identify behaviors or types of actions that are critical for a particular role based on analyzing the top performers in that role, or by having people affected by that role identify the top qualities associated with it. These tend to be more effective than the other assessments because they relate to specific aspects of how the job should be performed. However, they also have their drawbacks. They are time consuming and quite costly. Also, some assessments have resulted in as many as 70 competencies for a single role—far too many for the development of a clear and focused direction. Moreover, once the competencies are developed and we have a sense of where the strengths and weaknesses lie, we still have to return to basic development, coaching and training to upgrade those skills. If managers haven't been developing employees through coaching until now, an assessment is unlikely to change their behavior. If follow-up is weak, what happens when the organizational environment changes and, as a result, when the roles change accordingly?

There is the assumption that if everyone performs to their highest competency, the result will be a high-performing organization. While it is true that upgrading people's competencies helps lead to higher individual job performance, it is not clear that doing so develops a high-performing *organization*. The missing piece in the equation involves linkage and results. Competencies can describe behaviors of linkage, but cannot represent those linkages in terms of actual interdependencies and day to day performance. At one company, a competency for a manager's role was "Accountability," which was defined as "completing assignments on time." This is only a small part of accountability.

Accountability-Based® Assessment: Uncover the Truth in Motion

No assessment, regardless of how good it is, creates higher performance. It is easy and "comfortable" to spend lots of time assessing competencies, needs, attitudes, and aptitudes with the goal of determining what people should be doing differently. The challenge, however, is how to ensure that people take action on the areas that show up for improvement. Assessments of aptitude, skills or competencies do not always reveal or uncover the actual breakdowns in an organization. Rather they represent an attempt to improve organizational performance by improving people's skills. That a skill or competency is demonstrated effectively is no guarantee that it will be *applied* appropriately.

An accountability assessment is different from the others in that it directly identifies the pattern of breakdowns between departments, levels of management, and functions in the organization. These breakdowns represent performance and operational deficiencies that block the achievement of business outcomes in measurable ways. These breakdowns usually reveal themselves in repeated patterns that exist in various parts of the organization.

For instance, in a division of a large organization, the pattern breakdown was that middle managers would always take their conflicts to upper management for resolution. As a result, decisions weren't being made in a timely manner, and many conflicts weren't being resolved or even surfaced. It wasn't hard to trace the conflicts to duplication of effort, wasted resources, and project overruns, all of which relate to organizational performance. After changing the process for resolving conflict, and providing the managers with the skills for using the process effectively, productivity and responsiveness improved significantly and the division met its production goals for the first time in several years.

Another organization had tried to create more employee empowerment by directing middle management to stay out of the problems surfaced by their supervisors. "If a supervisor comes to you with a problem," they were told, "we want you to ignore them or direct them to solve it themselves." Over several months, more problem solving was indeed done by supervisors and their teams, but a major communication breakdown developed between middle management and the work teams. Cross-functional problems between supervisors were never surfaced or discussed because no process had been established to do so. Now "empowered," each supervisor tried to solve the problems in isolation. As a result, several teams would be working on the same projects without knowing it, wasting both human and technical resources. Breakdowns between supervisors and their teams went unnoticed since they were supposed to solve problems on their own without involvement of middle management. Interestingly enough, middle management's competencies around "empowering employees to solve problems on their own," "maintaining a global and strategic perspective," and "giving clear direction without micro-managing" all scored high on their competency evaluation. They even scored high on their problem solving abilities. However, the organization was breaking down because the linkage between middle managers and supervisors had been cut, and the problems weren't being surfaced to the appropriate level for resolution.

Because an accountability assessment addresses the actual breakdowns that are taking place in the organization, it must be continually updated and tied to the actual performance of the organization. This is the same way a top performing baseball team practices or a symphonic orchestra rehearses. They identify patterns of performance breakdowns and practice the improvement of those areas until the breakdowns are resolved. Sometimes it is a skills or process issue, but more often than not it is an issue of executing the process effectively using the skills that already exist.

As the organization evolves or the needs of customers change, new levels of execution are required and with these will likely come some new breakdowns. Because the accountability assessment is focused on actual patterns of breakdown, as the organization evolves, so, too, will the accountability assessment, continually identifying new changes that are needed. Regardless of how the organization is structured, or what roles exist within it, the accountability assessment brings the performance breakdowns to the surface where they can be translated into projects to improve dysfunctional processes, training to improve skills, and practice sessions to improve execution.

Terrific Training…But, Where's the Results?

What happens when a training program is finished? We expect the newly trained employees to go back to their workplace and apply their new skills to achieve better results. In some cases, managers attend an orientation session to become aware of the training so that they can support the newly trained employees. However, most managers believe that the employees are fully trained once they get back to the workplace. Consequently, they provide little coaching. Why should they? After all, the employee completed the training program!

In short, the only accountability that exists with regard to training comes at the end of the training program when the participants complete an evaluation. What's really being evaluated there is how much the participant *enjoyed* the training experience. There is no direct accountability for using the newly learned skills back in the workplace. Consequently, trainers strive to be as *entertaining* as possible. I know of one training company that promises its clients "enter*train*ment!" Trainers are reluctant to place participants in an environment in which they might be challenged too much because this might cause them to become angry or frustrated, causing them to complete a negative evaluation at the end of the training session. This is the way traditional training has evolved to become a "comfortable" experience, one that isn't accountable for improving results in the workplace.

Figures 10-1 and 10-2 demonstrate the relationship among all of the players involved in a training program—the trainers, the participants and management. Most of the time is spent perfecting the training program itself. Relatively little time is spent preparing managers to provide the monitoring, coaching, evaluation and recognition that is critical to sustain results. Managers attend a generic workshop on coaching skills and the expectation is that they will be able to apply those skills to every situation. Even if managers come away with some skill in coaching, no consistent system or process is in place for them to use their coaching skills relative to a particular training program. It doesn't take long before the day-to-day demands of the job take priority over the coaching of employees to improve their performance by integrating their newly developed skills.

There's a story about Clyde Drexler, an ex-basketball player for the Portland Trailblazers and Houston Rockets, who is the highest percentage shooter of free throws in the NBA. Still, he also has a personal coach just to develop his free throws. One of his fans asked a commentator why he had a coach when he was already the best. The commentator replied: "Maybe having a coach is one of the reasons he *is* the best."

Five Steps to Performance-Based Training with Accountability

Step 1: Clarify the Desired Business Results and Baseline Measurements

As with all accountability-based® approaches, it is critical to understand the desired business outcomes for the training program prior to its development. Too often, training is determined based on a means rather than an end: *We need team building,* or *We need better communication.* In both these cases, we don't know *why* we want team building or better communication. In other words, what *results* could be achieved if we had better teamwork or communication?

The desired business outcome for training can be derived from the accountability assessment, which identifies the breakdowns within the organization that were linked to preventing better business results. Focusing on the breakdowns not only gives us a clear outcome for improvement that addresses organizational performance, but also provides a baseline measurement from the assessment that we can use like a benchmark to demonstrate future measurable improvement. Ultimately, the effectiveness of the training is determined not by how well people like the program, but on the measurable improvement demonstrated after participants take action, receive coaching, and modify their actions based on results.

Step 2: Develop New Habits of Behavior

Next, identify the dysfunctional pattern of behavior that needs changing. Sometimes it is a process or system that needs to be developed or modified. For instance, perhaps projects are breaking down because the current process for managing a project is so cumbersome that no one uses it. Or maybe mistakes are staying "underground." That was the problem at one department I worked with that depended on the completion of technically based projects. Unfortunately, people were afraid to openly discuss problems or mistakes. Therefore, projects would be getting off-track and no one could help resolve the issues because no one was aware of them. All the project managers spent three days training to increase their project management skills, but still didn't have the safety to surface mistakes. Realizing that this wasn't due to a lack of skills, I set up a special problem-solving meeting where the sole purpose was to surface project problems and discuss them. We used the Interaction Agreement process discussed in Chapter 9 in order to establish the safety for managers to be open. This new process helped project managers overcome their fear of being reprimanded for mistakes (which turned out in any case to be unfounded), and to develop a new way to deal with problems and issues.

This step is particularly important because many problems blamed on a "lack of skills" have nothing to do with skills. How many times have you been trained on communication skills only to return to the workplace where there is a breakdown in the communication process due to role confusion or other issues unrelated to skills?

Step 3: Identify the Skills Necessary to Support the New Habit

Now we are in a position to identify the skills needed to execute the new process effectively. Sometimes people already have the skills and just need a refresher tailored to the context of the new process or system. Sometimes they may need more intensive skill building.

Do you remember learning how to ride a bicycle? Did you read a book or discuss riding a bike using a case study or situational exercise? Most of us learned to ride a bike by being guided on some basics and then getting on the bike and trying to ride. We lost our balance and fell, but we got up and rode again until we learned to ride on our own. When skills are taught, it is generally more effective to learn and apply them in a real life situation rather than in a hypothetical case study or in a situational exercise. This way we can experience the skill in a situation in which we can relate. For instance, we can practice conflict resolution skills by identifying *real* conflicts that need resolving, walking through the process, and sometimes even resolving those conflicts if both parties are present. When this happens, we not only learn the skill, we also gain confidence from applying it successfully. In addition, we complete real work that needs to be done, which gives us a high return on our investment of time.

Step 4: Develop the Accountability Linkage

When is skill building most likely to fail? Immediately upon conclusion of the training? Or a week later? Learning new skills involves learning new habits. This is true whether we are learning new methods for managing conflict, communicating, managing others, or making decisions. It is not just a skill that needs developing; it is a habit that needs changing. It is easier to apply the skill just after it's taught than it is to apply it a week later when old habits have already taken over. Thus, training in the classroom can rarely be sustained to achieve long-term results. Top performing athletes, musicians, and dancers all have coaches with whom they work after they have learned the basics of their skill. Coaching is critical for fine-tuning the application of a skill in a real workplace setting.

As illustrated by Figure 10-1, training is not an accountable process unless it involves an accountability linkage with the manager as a coach. Managers must be provided with a system for coaching employees to effectively apply their new skills on the job to get results. This system must include **monitoring** the employees' application of newly acquired skills; **coaching** them to fine-tune their application of skills; **evaluating** the effectiveness of the new skills in achieving improved performance; and **acknowledging** success when performance has been improved. Employees, with coaching by their managers, are accountable for improving performance to achieve the desired outcomes of the work unit and organization.

Figure 10-1: Training with Management Coaching

Step 5: Test the Program, Measure Results and Fine-Tune

Once the accountability-based® training program is designed, it must be piloted. The effectiveness of an accountability-based® training program is measured by the actual results that are achieved back in the workplace. These results must improve performance that achieves the business outcomes. If results aren't achieved, first the process (habit pattern) needs to be reviewed and fine-tuned to ensure that it is effective. Second, the skills of the participants need to be assessed to determine if they are adequate to perform the process.

Complete the Accountability Cycle

Myth: Employee development depends on identifying needs and competencies.

Truth: Employee development depends on identifying business outcomes and organizational breakdowns.

In the accountability-based® training program, employees are accountable to management for applying their new awareness and skills. Management is accountable to both upper management and the trainers for implementing a coaching system that will assist employees back on the job.

And what about the trainers? To whom are they accountable? Trainers are accountable to management for achieving those business outcomes that initiated the training program in the first place. But the trainers can be held accountable for their part of the process (the training) *only* if management is held equally accountable for their part (carrying out the coaching component).

The result is a fully linked system of accountability. Training takes place in a meaningful context in which measurable and meaningful improvement can and should be expected to take place. Any dysfunctional problems discovered in the accountability assessment should be minimized or eliminated based on the implementation of effective training.

Figure 10-2: Accountability-Based® Training

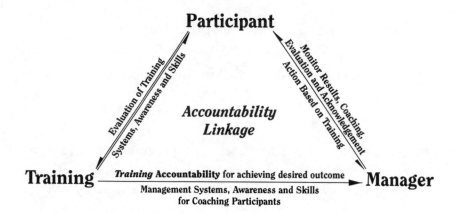

∽ **11** ∽

Get Started:
Your Next Steps to Get
Breakthrough Results

A few years ago I called on a potential client who wanted help developing a more accountable organization. He described his organization as having a highly skilled work force, but one that didn't complete projects on time and was paralyzed by competitive territorialism. I asked him what the costs were to these problems and he responded that their market share was declining and they weren't able to enter new markets due to their lack of responsiveness. As a result, they were in a constant state of crisis.

Together we outlined an approach that required his team of twenty-five senior and middle managers to meet for a two-day session to begin addressing these problems. However, this leader could never find the time for us to meet. He had too many crises to deal with. I suggested we meet on a weekend, but he didn't want to inconvenience his staff. After trying in vain for two months to schedule our session, I decided that his commitment (and pain) wasn't high enough for him to invest the time it would take to make a difference. A year later, he called me back. Now, as a result of downsizing, only a third of his organization remained. Now he was even clearer about the need to take action and about the costs of not doing so, and he was prepared to finally commit to taking the actions necessary to improve his organization.

While we may sense the need to increase the level of accountability in our organization and to improve the quality and effectiveness of our performance, we often don't have the commitment level to begin investing time and resources to making a difference. Getting started can be the most challenging part of creating an accountable organization.

Below are the six steps for putting the process in motion for developing an accountable organization. These are the steps required in order to begin making the necessary changes to improve performance that will achieve business goals, and respond to the changes brought on by our customers, our competition and by technological advancements.

Step 1: Clarify Business Outcomes and Intention

Before we can clarify our business outcomes we must understand the scope of our influence. Is our influence organizational, divisional, departmental, work unit or individual? Based on the scope of our influence, we can identify the external drivers that have an impact on us. For instance, if we have an *organizational* influence, our external drivers are generated from outside factors impacting the *organization*. If we have a *work unit* sphere of influence, our external drivers are generated from factors outside of our *work unit*, which includes our department, our division, the rest of the organization *plus* factors outside of the organization itself.

Then we must identify our business goals and prioritize them based on our external drivers. Together, our goals and external drivers provide the context for understanding and determining our business outcomes. For example, one work unit had the following external drivers impacting its need for change:

Organizational External Drivers (Example)
- Increased competition especially in terms of price and quality service
- Customers demanding more responsiveness

Divisional External Factors (Example)
- New leadership
- Implementation of new computer system

Departmental External Factors (Example)
- Cost cutting
- Restructuring of the department
- Potential downsizing

Based on their goals to implement a new computer system (in keeping with the implementation plan for the division), they developed the business outcomes to maximize customer responsiveness during the time that the new computer system was being implemented. Their next step was to create a clear intention, based on their desired business outcome and on their internal values of team support, flexibility, and responsiveness.

Their expressed intention was to implement a new computer system that was invisible to the customer. To fulfill this intention, they committed to cross-train each other in areas of customer service, and to coordinate their response to customers such that a seamless work unit was ensured. Finally, they agreed to support one another with respect to fears of downsizing, of changes in job function and of having to learn the new computer system. As a result, the team members were clear about the purpose of the changes they would be making, the support they would be providing one another, their roles in the change, and their relationship with their customers.

Step 2: Conduct an Accountability Assessment

People frequently skip this stage, jumping immediately to strategies and goals in an attempt to quickly respond to external conditions or to quickly achieve their bottom line success. Invariably, their strategies and goals will be undermined by the skipping of this key step which identifies dysfunctional patterns of behavior.

An accountability assessment determines which patterns of management and employee behavior are keeping the organization stuck in its old paradigm. These patterns include communications (up, down, and across the organization), how non-performance is handled, how decisions are made, how conflicts are resolved, and how projects are managed. Ultimately, this assessment will identify where linkages are broken between the different levels within the organization and between the different functions within the organization. These broken links are what impede responsiveness to external drivers and, ultimately, achievement of the desired business outcomes.

An accountability assessment needs to be customized based on the scope of influence determined in Step 1. When the accountability assessment is focused on the organization, it identifies more macro patterns of behavior. It might show, for example, how information flows between senior management and upper middle management. When the accountability assessment is focused on the work unit, it identifies the interrelationships between the manager and the team. It might indicate how decisions are made among the team members to ensure accountability of all affected team members.

The work unit used as an example in Step 1 discovered in their accountability assessment that the team didn't have a clear process for resolving conflict or an agreement requiring them to go to each other to discuss and resolve conflicts that surface. As a result, they had several unresolved conflicts, a lack of trust among team members, and various cliques. Until this problem was resolved, they would be unable to complete the cross training, develop the supportive relationships to deal with the pressures of change, learn new technology, or maintain their responsiveness to customers.

Step 3: Determine the Approach for Involving Employees in a Change Effort

In most change efforts the strategy of involvement is based on a philosophy. Some philosophies insist that all changes are top-down. Others say bottom-up. And some recommend a team method.

An accountability-based® approach to organizational change depends on the situation. The choice of strategy is based not on a philosophy but on the business outcomes, the dysfunctional patterns of the organization, and the specific characteristics of the organization. Different types of industries have different types of organizations, which require different strategies. Health care organizations have different characteristics than manufacturing or educational organizations. The history of the organization influences which strategy should be used. Organizations that have experienced a lot of change or skill development will require a different strategy from those that have experienced little change. Operational constraints that affect productivity and quality will also influence the manner in which change should be introduced. Generally, we've found the following to be true:

- **Top-down** implementation is well suited to a situation in which management is required to upgrade their level of leadership to support restructuring, re-engineering, or other change efforts. When the organization is paralyzed by lack of communication, coordination, or sharing of information among departments, it is important to start the effort with management. Also, when management has not taken care of their basic role of managing performance, making decisions, coaching and developing their staff, a top-down approach is necessary. Finally, when the organization is either moving from entitlement to individual accountability, or from cross-functional accountability to organizational accountability, a top-down approach is usually best. *This approach develops cross-functional managers into a leadership team aligned for the purpose of accomplishing organizational priorities and changing the culture to ensure organizational success.*

- **Bottom-up** implementation is well suited to a grass roots effort or as an empowerment approach to create a mass effort to transition from a culture of blame and denial to one of accountable action and behavior. This strategy of change is necessary in the case where an increase in customer satisfaction is required. Here, it becomes critical to directly include management in a bottom-up approach to change. Without strong, direct linkage, change efforts are short lived or sabotaged by misunderstanding and miscommunication. *This approach links employees to management with a structured coaching and acknowledgment system based on the awareness and skills presented during the intervention.*

• A **team-based** approach is best used when there is a targeted change effort based on restructuring cross-functional and functional teams, or when the organization is moving toward greater self-direction. Often, when there has already been a lot of training and people are skilled in the basics of leadership, communication, project management, and conflict resolution, it is appropriate to use a team-based approach which is less skill-based and more of a working session intervention. Also, when measurable results are needed in a short period of time, a team-based approach to change is the most effective. *This approach develops teams in working sessions that deal with real workplace performance and relationship issues developing clear performance measures tied to business outcomes.*

The work unit used as an example in Steps 1 and 2 chose a team-based approach to change. This was based on the scope of change, the need for fast results, and the breakdowns in the interrelationships between employees themselves and between the manager and employees.

Step 4: Develop a Strategic Operational Plan for Improvement

Once the approach to change is developed, it is crucial to plan the *operational* aspects of the transformation. It is often important to translate the business outcomes and dysfunctional patterns of behavior into a set of "success factors" which provide a blueprint for success against which the transformation may be measured. Once the success factors are clear, it is important to plan the timing of the implementation based on the organizational constraints created from other projects, the business cycle itself, and other factors involving the limitation of resources. For instance, it is generally a poor idea to plan a major intervention for a retail clothing store during the month of December since customer demand is extremely high during that period. Any coordination considerations (including coverage of positions, scheduling, and location arrangements) must also be determined at this point.

Finally, the plan must be translated into a set of milestones with dates that can be tracked. The milestones must be clear and visible for easy tracking and review. No matter what strategy or decisions are made about the details, it should be reviewed for the impact it will have on the business outcomes and on the identified dysfunctional patterns of behavior. After determining the milestones, then any potential obstacles to success should be pinpointed, and "recovery" strategies put in place to mobilize resources and respond to the obstacles. Finally, a plan for tracking progress according to the milestones should be implemented to ensure success.

Step 5: Develop a Communication Strategy

Communication is one of the key steps to success. In developing the strategy we must consider the audience receiving the information and plan the most effective way to deliver the message. The messengers, the modes of communication of the message, and the timing of the communication relative to organizational constraints should all be considered.

Included must be a process for on-going communication during the implementation so that people are kept informed of the progress and results of the transformation, and reminded of the transformation's purpose and context. Watch out for the trap of trying to SELL the transformation. It makes people suspicious. Instead, provide a *clear context* for the transformation—an understanding of why the transformation is taking place—*and then involve people in action as soon as possible*.

This is accomplished by first reviewing for them the purpose of the organization itself, and then providing them with a history of the non-negotiable external conditions that affected the organization five years ago, those that currently affect the organization, and finally those that have been anticipated to affect the organization in the future. This will produce a trend of non-negotiable external factors to which the organization must respond to in order to survive or to stay competitive. *This trend is the "context" for the transformation.*

Next, communicate the organization's internal values, stressing the ways in which the organization's behaviors have, in the past, changed in order to achieve those *unchanging* values in the face of *changing* and non-negotiable external conditions.

Then point out the dysfunctional behavior that currently exists in the organization and which needs to be changed in order to respond effectively to these external drivers.

Finally, communicate to people at all levels and all functions the *call to action* to overcome the dysfunctional patterns of behavior standing in the way of achieving organizational success.

Step 6: Measure and Recognize Results

Between three and six months after the beginning of implementation, you must evaluate actual measurable results to discover what is working and what isn't working at moving the company toward the desired business outcomes. This is the time when people get discouraged either because they don't feel the change is making a difference or because they are frustrated that it isn't producing results fast enough. Generally, the measurable results (once taken) exceed people's expectations. This becomes a motivational factor in maintaining their focus on the transformation and even in increasing their willingness to take more action. Also, this is the time to acknowledge the people or teams who have made a special effort to be successful. The conclusion of this step is inspiring and rewarding. We all want to make a difference and to know that our efforts are meaningful and valued.

❧ Final Thoughts ❧

Achieving breakthrough results in half the time requires courage, perseverance and the commitment to endure until the end. The people in the organizations described in this book all had the courage to "step outside the box" of their roles and expectations to achieve a new standard of excellence. While I was fortunate to have had the opportunity to work with many of them, they are the true pioneers. They risked the security of the status quo to make a difference that would contribute to the lives of their co-workers and employees, and enhance the services received by their customers.

Developing a culture of accountability can be challenging. It requires care and thoughtful consideration. At first, you may find yourself confronting many popular ideas about leadership. You will need courage, belief and an intention to sustain you as you move your thinking beyond current paradigms. Then you will be called upon to engage others in your intention. This means painting a compelling picture with probable outcomes that you cannot really prove, but that you can make tangible through your conviction, your clarity, and your willingness to take risks.

Finally, after you have given great thought to making a meaningful difference—creating a breakthrough—and sharing your intention with others who will be affected, you must ultimately take action. It is in your action that you make a true difference. Remember that your actions need not be perfect, but must include recovery processes that support you in observing and modifying your approach as you progress. During those times when everything appears to be going wrong, you must rely on your commitment, your intention and your support system to see you through. Ultimately, you can do it and, if you have the desire, you will do it!

You do not have to do it alone. You can join the Accountability Network, tapping into the resources of many others who are committed to developing accountable organizations that achieve breakthrough results. Whether you have a success to share or a challenge with which you would like guidance or support, please feel free to contact me personally to be connected with a network of experienced colleagues from several organizations, who are dedicated to making a difference.

This book was written for you. I hope that reading it has given you some new ideas. The concepts and techniques I have shared here have been proven to work for others, and I believe they will work for you.

Although this is the concluding chapter of this book, it is not an ending, but a beginning, which will be added onto by people like you who are finding new paths and making differences that are meaningful for everyone involved.

It is critical for all of us to be dedicated to discovering the new truths of leadership that will take us into the future. We all must participate in creating organizations, communities and homes that reflect the values of integrity, accountability and growth which advance our experience of service, morale and quality to achieve breakthrough results. Through such efforts, working will regain its value as a worthwhile and rewarding human endeavor of making meaningful contributions while generating healthy profits, instead of continuing its decline into the mere pursuit of power and short-term financial gain.

◌ **References** ◌

This book could not have been written without the support and guidance of many other authors who have created a path of knowledge and experience on which to base my work. While I have formed my models, strategies and techniques according to my own experience, there are also many others who are paving the way for the future with their own ideas and experiences. Hopefully, as you continue as a pioneer for improving organizations and yourself, you can use these great minds and their works to move you forward just as I have. While this isn't a complete list of useful references, it is a good starting point from which to expand our consciousness and ideas.

1. *Beyond Reengineering: How the Process-Centered Organization is Changing Our Work and Our Lives*, by Michael Hammer, Harper & Row, 1996.

2. *Building Your Company's Vision*, by James C. Collins and Jerry I. Porras, Harvard Business Review, September 1, 1996.

3. *Built to Last: Successful Habits of Visionary Companies*, by James C. Collins and Jerry I. Porras, Harper & Row, 1997.

4. *Corporate Lifecycles: How and Why Corporations Grow and Die and What to Do About It*, by Ichak Adizes, Prentice Hall, 1988.

5. *Danger in the Comfort Zone*, by Judith M. Bardwick, American Management Association, 1991.

6. *Driving Fear Out of the Workplace*, by Kathleen D. Ryan and Daniel K. Oestreich, Jossey-Bass, 1998.

7. *Even Eagles Need a Push: Learning to Soar in a Changing World*, by David McNally, Dell Publishing, 1990.

8. *Jack Welch Speaks: Wisdom from the World's Greatest Business Leader*, by Janet Lowe, John Wiley & Sons, Inc., 1998.

9. *Leaders: The Strategies for Taking Charge*, by Warren Bennis and Burt Nanus, Harper & Row Publishers, Inc., 1985.

10. *Leadership and the One Minute Manager*, by Kenneth Blanchard, Ph.D., Patricia Zigarmi, Ed.D., and Drea Zigarmi, Ed.D., William Morrow and Company, Inc., 1985.

11. *Leadership is an Art*, by Max DePree, Doubleday, 1989.

12. *Leadership Jazz*, by Max DePree, Dell Publishing, 1992.

13. *Liberating the Corporate Soul: Building a Visionary Organization*, by Richard Barrett, Butterworth-Heinemann, 1998.

14. *Spiritual Warrior: The Art of Living a Spiritual Life*, by John-Roger, Mandeville Press, 1998.

15. *The Age of Paradox*, by Charles Handy, Harvard Business School Press, 1994.

16. *The Balanced Scorecard: Translating Strategy into Action*, by Robert S. Kaplan and David P. Norton, Harvard Business School Press, 1996.

17. *The Corporate Mystic*, by Gay Hendricks, Ph.D. and Kate Ludeman, Ph.D., Bantam Books, 1996.

18. *The Empowered Manager*, by Peter Block, Jossey-Bass Publishers, Inc., 1987.

19. *The Fifth Discipline*, by Peter Senge, Currency Doubleday, 1990.

20. *The Great Game of Business*, by Jack Stack, Currency Doubleday, 1994.

21. *The Leadership Challenge: How to Keep Getting Extraordinary Things Done in Organizations*, by James M. Kouzes and Barry Z. Posner, Jossey-Bass Publishers, 1995.

22. *The Seven Habits of Highly Effective People*, by Stephen R. Covey, Simon and Schuster, 1989.

23. *The Seven Spiritual Laws of Success: A Practical Guide to the Fulfillment of Your Dreams*, by Deepak Chopra, Amber-Allen Publishing and New World Library, 1993.

24. *The Tao of Personal Leadership*, by Diane Dreher, Harper & Row, 1996.

25. *Thriving on Chaos: Handbook for a Management Revolution*, by Tom Peters, HarperPerennial, 1987.

26. *Wordpower*, by Edward de Bono. Penguin, 1990.

∽ The Accountability Network ∽

THE ACCOUNTABILITY NETWORK is an active, responsive and growing group of talented CEOs, managers, change agents and employees who have embraced the power of accountability. We correspond via an interactive email and web-based system to share new ideas, old truths, and support one another through on-line fellowship and information exchange.

To participate, just send an email to *accountability@impaqcorp.com* or contact us at our website at *www.impaqcorp.com*.

❦ About the Author ❧

Like other consultants in the 1970s, Mark Samuel recognized the shortcomings inherent with traditional OD efforts. Unlike the rest, Mark developed a *different approach* to training, consulting and organizational change:

Accountability-Based® Improvement Systems.

Mark rightly assessed that, unless there was an attack to change the culture, any skill-based training would simply reinforce the (troubled) environment already in place. What is needed is an environment where people have the safety to take risks, where recovery – not perfection – is planned and where people can "count on each other."

Accountability became the banner through which results would flow. And flow they have – often achieving TWICE the results in HALF the time. In fact, the company name was changed to "IMPAQ®" because client after client would share that "you have no idea the *impact* you've had on our organization…". We were told this so often by so many we believed there was a message in it for us.

Mark has become the loudest proponent of creating accountable cultures. "It is simply the fastest, most effective way to develop an organization that thrives on innovation, teamwork and response to customers."

Mark continues to consult, train and present for clients and organizations. You may obtain a list of Mark's current speaking schedule by contacting the IMPAQ® corporate office **800.332.2251**, or visiting the website at **www.impaqcorp.com**—for more direct contact, Mark invites you to communicate using his email: **marks@impaqcorp.com**

❦ About IMPAQ® ❦

IMPAQ® IS AN ORGANIZATIONAL IMPROVEMENT COMPANY that has been developing organizational accountability since 1987. Many Fortune 500 corporations and emerging businesses have achieved breakthrough results and consistent success using the strategies and systems discussed in this book.

IMPAQ® specializes in:

- Team Systems
- Culture Change
- Leadership Development
- Employee Orientation
- Executive Coaching
- Public Workshops on Performance Consulting

Tools to Improve Accountability & Performance

The Accountability Revolution—
Achieve Breakthrough Results in Half the Time!

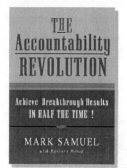

After twenty+ years of consulting, training and coaching...after creating and pioneering Account-ability-Based® technologies...after establishing and building an organizational consulting firm with a proven record of achieving results...after building a clientele straight from the Fortune 500....

Mark Samuel has finally written the definitive primer on accountability: *What it is. How to keep it. How to grow it. What it will do for you, and everyone around you.*

The Accountability Revolution is a must-have for every individual wanting to know the key to achieving and sustaining high performance...and the key to IMPAQ®'s breakthrough results!

Team Interaction Questionnaire

An easy, effective tool for producing measurable improvement in team performance and relation-ships.

The *Team Interaction Questionnaire* can be used as an integrated part of any high-performance team system. Because of its simplicity and easy-to-use design, it is ideal for:

- Team Development Sessions
- Identifying Cross-Functional Team Needs
- Identifying Leadership Team Strengths and Weaknesses
- Group Interventions Including Dysfunctional Teams
- Improving Team Meetings

This tool is popular because it takes very little time to complete and it is confidential. A team can learn to use it as an ongoing tool for development and measurement of team success. Its simple scoring can also be recorded by using the self-contained executable form files.

Success through Accountability—A 2-Hour Module

Here is the way to get your employees "on the same page." Building personal accountability not only increases performance and satisfaction but it directly relates to organizational results!

Success Through Accountability is a highly interactive program designed for new hires and existing employees who are experiencing a change in their role. This powerful program will easily fit into your existing Orientation Program. It takes only 1° to 2 hours and provides tangible tools for entering the workplace with a clear intention of being accountable, taking initiative, and improving teamwork. It can be delivered in a large or small group, or one-on-one.

Employees of all ages and years of experience can relate to this program and use it to improve their performance and communication in the workplace.

Card-Sized Accountability

Now you can take it with you! We have captured the Personal Accountability Model on one side and added the 5-Steps to Breakthrough on the reverse side...and we've placed it all on a card no larger than your average credit card. Hard, durable plastic with a thick, protective laminate means this pocket or wallet tool will last for years to come. Ideal for organizational promotions.

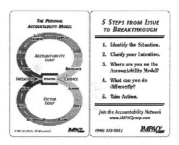

Situational Action Inventory— A Personal Accountability Assessment

Because accountability is at the heart of an organization's ability to respond to change, knowing upon which strand of the accountability ladder your employees stand is key to personal and organizational improvement. It has been proven that increasing organizational accountability results in measurable improvements - including higher performance, increased productivity, faster response to change, and greater customer satisfaction.

The *Situational Action Inventory* is a self scoring assessment to determine the degree to which your employees can be counted on. Managers and non-managers alike are given a series of solutions to common workplace challenges. These aggregate responses determine the degree to which they are accountable, as well as the areas in which they can become more accountable.

A comprehensive, self-assessment that delivers Individual Awareness, Education, Coaching and Action Planning, the *SAI* identifies specific actions for contribution and improvement. This tool is flexible enough to be used with Individual Performance Coaching, in a Team-Building session, for Hiring & Placement, as a New Employee Orientation and as an Organizational Culture Assessment.

Team Performance Profile

By focusing on eight critical success dimensions for excellent team performance, the **Team Performance Profile** will create a picture of your current team member perceptions and behaviors as well as highlight team strengths and areas in need of improvement. This tool allows teams to utilize current strengths in focusing upon strategic improvement efforts, which increases the return on investment. After completing individual profiles, team members will be able to see how their thinking matches up to the group consensus.

Also available with a consultative response, The *TPP* may be individually reviewed by an IMPAQ® Senior Consultant who will provide a written response, complete with a custom evaluation and specific recommendations.

Pocket Trainers

Some of the more popular tools for participants of IMPAQ® implementations are our Pocket Trainers— Pocket-sized Memory Joggers containing the key models and strategies from the training session just completed. You won't need to reference the training manual for those dynamic change tools and models when you've got the Pocket Trainers...they "keep on teaching long after the session ends."

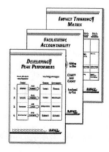

Poster: **IMPAQ®***'s Personal Accountability Model*

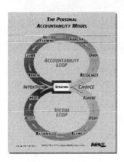

Probably our most recognizable identification, other than our logo, is IMPAQ®'s Accountability Model. A foundational model representing the progressive levels of behavior, the Victim/Accountability Model has a proven record of promoting performance improvement. Now available for the first time as a wall-mountable poster, this four-color Personal Accountability Model is a great tool for use in Team meetings for helping team members get "unstuck" and move forward.

For more information on these products and future tools to assist you, please contact us through our website: **www.impaqcorp.com**, or call us toll-free at **(800) 332-2251**.

❧ Index ☙

A

Accountability
  anatomy of 13
  assessment
    203–205, 207, 211, 216–217
  Continuum 26, 29, 86, 174
  developing a culture of 223–225
  Five Levels of 25–29
    1: Entitlement 27
    2: Individual 27–28
    3: Work Unit 28
    4: Cross-Functional 28–29
    5: Organizational 29
    summary chart 30

  interlocking 13, 16, 191–195
  linkage 122–123, 169, 190, 209
  Network 224–225
  personal 107
  Revolution 18, 24–25, 234

Accountability Network 224

Accountability-Based® Implementation
  122
  Six Stages of 122–141
    1: Planning the Implementation and
      Communication Strategy 124–130
    2: Accountability-Based® Implementation
      131–133
    3: Clarifying Roles and Relationships 133–135
    4: Tracking Milestones and Making Modifications
      135–136
    5: Communicating Results 136–140
    6: Recognizing Success and the People Involved
      140–141

Assessment
  10–11, 14, 29, 139, 173,
  200–204, 207, 211, 216, 217
  Accountability-Based® 202
  Tools
    Situational Action Inventory
    235–236

B

Bank of America 3

Blaming
  23, 37, 45, 55, 63, 77, 81, 83,
  89, 107, 167

Breakthrough results
  1, 40, 46, 50, 79, 91, 121, 148,
  167, 170–171, 213, 223–224,
  233–234

Business outcomes
  35–39, 46, 48, 50, 52, 83,
  86–88, 90, 93, 109–114, 119,
  140–141, 165, 174, 199, 203,
  206, 210–211, 214–221

Buy-in
  11, 51, 123, 143, 146–161, 185
  vs. Involvement 151–152
  when it is a trap 147–149
  when it is appropriate 152–154

C

Cadence Design Systems 8

Change
  adjusting to 131–132
  communicating
    11, 39, 76, 87–88, 110–112,
    130, 146–147
  culture 115, 122, 141
  discouragement after
    15, 124, 133, 136–138
  executives 81, 84
  fear of 67, 125–126
  how to move through 76–77
  managing 3